Bullying

Series Editor: Cara Acred

Volume 304

Independence Educational Publishers

First published by Independence Educational Publishers

The Studio, High Green

Great Shelford

Cambridge CB22 5EG

England

ISBN-13: 978 1 86168 749 4

Printed in Great Britain

Zenith Print Group

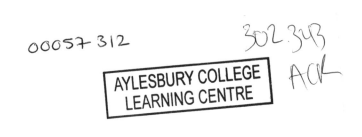

Contents

Introduction

Bullying is Volume 304 in the **ISSUES** series. The aim of the series is to offer current, diverse information about important issues in our world, from a UK perspective.

ABOUT BULLYING

The Center for Disease Control says that students who are bullied are more likely to suffer from low self-esteem and even experience physical symptoms such as headaches and sleep problems. But it's not just children who are at risk of being bullied; this book explores the many forms that bullying can take, including workplace bullying, cyberbullying, homophobic bullying and bullying at school. It also considers the different ways of tackling bullying.

OUR SOURCES

Titles in the **ISSUES** series are designed to function as educational resource books, providing a balanced overview of a specific subject.

The information in our books is comprised of facts, articles and opinions from many different sources, including:

⇨ Newspaper reports and opinion pieces

⇨ Website factsheets

⇨ Magazine and journal articles

⇨ Statistics and surveys

⇨ Government reports

⇨ Literature from special interest groups.

A NOTE ON CRITICAL EVALUATION

Because the information reprinted here is from a number of different sources, readers should bear in mind the origin of the text and whether the source is likely to have a particular bias when presenting information (or when conducting their research). It is hoped that, as you read about the many aspects of the issues explored in this book, you will critically evaluate the information presented.

It is important that you decide whether you are being presented with facts or opinions. Does the writer give a biased or unbiased report? If an opinion is being expressed, do you agree with the writer? Is there potential bias to the 'facts' or statistics behind an article?

ASSIGNMENTS

In the back of this book, you will find a selection of assignments designed to help you engage with the articles you have been reading and to explore your own opinions. Some tasks will take longer than others and there is a mixture of design, writing and research-based activities that you can complete alone or in a group.

FURTHER RESEARCH

At the end of each article we have listed its source and a website that you can visit if you would like to conduct your own research. Please remember to critically evaluate any sources that you consult and consider whether the information you are viewing is accurate and unbiased.

Useful weblinks

www.acas.org.uk

www.anti-bullyingalliance.org.uk

www.bristol.ac.uk

www.bulliesout.com

www.bullying.co.uk

www.childline.org.uk

www.childnet.com

www.theconversation.com

www.cybersmile.org

www.ditchthelabel.org

www.executivesecretary.com

www.familylives.org.uk

www.gov.uk

www.healthandsafetyatwork.com

www.huffingtonpost.co.uk

www.mencap.org.uk

www.nhs.uk

www.nspcc.org.uk

www.psychologytoday.com

www.telegraph.co.uk

www2.warwick.ac.uk

Are you being bullied?

Bullying can happen to anyone and it's not always easy to recognise if it is happening to you. Read the questions below and see which ones you think may apply to you:

⇨ Does anyone make nasty comments to or about you?

⇨ Are you being called hurtful names?

⇨ Are you being made fun of for how you look or act?

⇨ Do you feel alone or isolated at school?

⇨ Has anyone spread spiteful and/ or untrue rumours about you?

⇨ Are you purposely excluded from a group?

⇨ Has anyone physically hurt you on purpose?

⇨ Have any of your personal belongings been purposely damaged?

⇨ Do you feel constantly harassed at school?

⇨ Do you ever feel that someone you believed to be a friend is trying to control you?

⇨ Has anyone ever posted or shared something about you online without your permission?

⇨ Do you ever receive nasty e-mails and/or text messages?

⇨ Has anyone pretended to be you on a social media site?

⇨ Do you ever feel anxious and afraid about going to school?

The more questions you answer yes to, the more likely it is you are being bullied. The first thing to understand is noone deserves to be bullied and you have the right to be safe. Secondly, you are not alone. There are people who are able to help you. Thirdly, it is important to talk to a trusted adult and tell them what has been going on.

What you can do

Remember, no one can make you feel bad about yourself without your consent. Don't allow anything the bully says about you to take root in your mind. If you allow this to happen, you will believe them and be robbed of your self-confidence and the bully would have won

Once you have identified who you would like to speak to (parent, teacher, close friend, sibling, etc.), it will be important to have all the details to tell/show them – what has been happening, who was involved, where did the bullying take place.

You can download and print the Bullying Incident Log and Plan from the Bullies Out website.

The document includes three steps:

Step 1: Describe the bullying that has been happening to you. Include dates, location, who is involved and details of the behaviour.

Step 2: Describe what you would like done about it. Think about how the situation could be stopped or prevented.

Step 3: What steps can you take to make that happen? Include who could help, what they can do, and what you can do.

Remember, if you are being bullied, it is not your fault and it is never your responsibility to make it stop; however, it is important that you take a stand – and learning to advocate for yourself is important. By thinking through a plan you will have a voice in the solution.

⇨ The above information is reprinted with kind permission from BulliesOut. Please visit www.bulliesout.com for further information.

© BulliesOut 2016

Leroy's story

By Leroy Binns

My name is Leroy, I have got a learning disability and I have personally experienced bullying.

Words hurt

Some people have called me "retard" and "mongol", which is not right or fair for someone with a learning disability.

The thing that I do not like is sometimes they have children with them, which means if they hear one of their parents say it they will think that it is OK for them to say it too.

Some children have even called me names like "spastic" or even "stupid", which I know that I am not – I have a had a job for 16 years! I do not blame the children because they do not know any better and it is what they have heard their parents say.

On the way home

One night on the way home from working the night shift at the warehouse company I worked for, I went to a takeaway place to get something to eat. On my way home I saw two men at the bus stop, as I turned into my road one of them stole my food.

I went back to the takeaway place and told them what happened, the man in the shop went out to see if he could see them and they gave me some more food. When I got home I told my mum what happened and she rang the police. The police came and took my statement. They also put something about what happened in my local paper, the *Islington Gazette*.

At the arcade

I am such a trusting person, once I was playing on a fruit machine, I was winning and a guy said that he would change it up for me. Stupidly I trusted him to do that but he did not turn up with the money.

So I went up to the cash desk to get it but they did not have it. They had a CCTV photo of him walking out of the arcade with the money.

They rang the police and the next morning I had to go to Tottenham police station to give them a statement.

At school

When I was younger I went to a special school. At play time a so-called friend of mine kept bullying me into giving him my money. I told one of the teachers so he stopped for a little while, but then he started again. This time he said that if I told anyone at school he would make it worse for me. There were times when I did not want to go to school because of him but I knew that I had to because I did not want my mum to get in trouble.

I could not tell my mum about him because I knew that she would have gone down to the school and I did not want her to do that because she had my other five younger brothers and sisters to look after.

In the end I went to the headmaster and he took him up in the office and said that bullying will not be tolerated at this school, he said that if it happens again he will be sent home. So he stopped and we become good friends after that.

Forgiving the bullies

I feel very upset and annoyed about what has happened to me but I do forgive those who have bullied me. I believe they didn't know any better and in time I think they will realise that what they did was not right.

18 November 2015

⇨ The above information is reprinted with kind permission from Mencap. Please visit www.mencap.org.uk for further information.

The Annual Bullying Survey 2015: UK bullying statistics 2015

The Annual Bullying Survey 2015 is one of the UK's most comprehensive reports into the bullying of young people. In partnership with 73 schools and colleges across the UK, our survey of over 4,800 young people highlights the current climate of bullying amongst 13–20-year-olds. Our complimentary report comes with tips and advice for schools, colleges, parents and guardians, the Government and young people on how you can help reduce the effect and prominence of bullying within your environment.

"43% of young people have been bullied, 44% of which are bullied at least once a week."

Key findings

⇨ 50% of young people have bullied another person, 30% of which do it at least once a week.

⇨ 69% of young people have witnessed somebody else being bullied, 43% of which see it at least once a week.

⇨ 43% of young people have been bullied, 44% of which are bullied at least once a week.

⇨ Appearance is cited as the number one aggressor of bullying, with 51% saying they were bullied because of attitudes towards how they look.

⇨ 26% said their weight was targeted, 21% body shape, 18% clothing, 14% facial features, 9% glasses and 8% hair colour.

⇨ 23% of females with ginger hair cited their hair colour as the bullying aggressor.

⇨ Overall, 47% of young people want to change their appearance. 48% want teeth whitening, 17% breast implants, 6% liposuction and 5% Botox.

⇨ 74% of those who have been bullied, have, at some point, been physically attacked. 17% have been sexually assaulted. 62% have been cyber bullied.

⇨ As a result of bullying, 29% self-harmed, 27% skipped class, 14% developed an eating disorder and 12% ran away from home.

⇨ Highest risk to bullying were the following groups: all types of disability, LGBT and low-income backgrounds.

"23% of females with ginger hair cited their hair colour as the bullying aggressor."

⇨ 40% of respondents reported being bullied for personal appearance, 36% reported being bullied for body shape, size and weight.

"Of those who were bullied, 98% were bullied by another student."

⇨ Of those who were bullied, 98% were bullied by another student, 17% from a sibling, 13% from a teacher and 8% from their parents/guardians.

⇨ 55% reporting bullying. 92% to a teacher, 49% were satisfied. 86% to a family member, 82% were satisfied. 69% to a friend, 72% were satisfied.

⇨ 45% did not report bullying. 32% of which felt it would not be taken seriously, 32% were too embarrassed and 26% were scared of it getting worse.

⇨ Those who have bullied were more likely to be in trouble with the police (36%) vs witnesses to bullying (23%) and those who have been bullied (22%).

⇨ The above information is reprinted with kind permission from Ditch The Label. Please visit www.ditchthelabel.org for further information.

Bullying at school

The law

Some forms of bullying are illegal and should be reported to the police. These include:

⇨ violence or assault

⇨ theft

⇨ repeated harassment or intimidation, e.g. name calling, threats and abusive phone calls, e-mails or text messages

⇨ hate crimes.

Schools and the law

By law, all state (not private) schools must have a behaviour policy in place that includes measures to prevent all forms of bullying among pupils.

This policy is decided by the school. All teachers, pupils and parents must be told what it is.

Anti-discrimination law

Schools must also follow anti-discrimination law. This means staff must act to prevent discrimination, harassment and victimisation within the school. This applies to all schools in England and Wales, and most schools in Scotland.

Northern Ireland has different anti-discrimination law.

Reporting bullying

You should report bullying to your school in the first place – or someone you trust if it happens outside school, e.g. in a club or online.

Tell the police if the bullying involves a crime.

Schools – reporting bullying

School staff will deal with bullying in different ways, depending on how serious the bullying is.

They might deal with it in school, e.g. by disciplining bullies, or they might report it to the police or social services.

Any discipline must take account of special educational needs or disabilities that the pupils involved may have.

Police – reporting bullying

Anyone can make a complaint to the police about bullying but it's usually a good idea to speak to your school first.

If you're reporting cyberbullying, keep a record of the date and time of the calls, e-mails or texts – don't delete any messages you receive.

Where to get help and advice

There are lots of organisations that provide support and advice if you're worried about bullying:

⇨ Anti-Bullying Alliance

⇨ Bullying UK

⇨ Childline

⇨ The Diana Award

⇨ Kidscape.

Bullying outside school

Head teachers have the legal power to make sure pupils behave outside of school premises (state schools only).

This includes bullying that happens anywhere off the school premises, e.g. on public transport or in a town centre.

School staff can also choose to report bullying to the police or local council.

Bullying – a definition

There is no legal definition of bullying.

However, it's usually defined as behaviour that is:

⇨ repeated

⇨ intended to hurt someone either physically or emotionally

⇨ often aimed at certain groups, e.g. because of race, religion, gender or sexual orientation.

It takes many forms and can include:

⇨ physical assault

⇨ teasing

⇨ making threats

⇨ name calling

⇨ cyberbullying – bullying via mobile phone or online (e.g. e-mail, social networks and instant messenger).

⇨ The above information is reprinted with kind permission from GOV.UK. Please visit www.gov.uk for further information.

Cyberbullying and digital abuse

The effects of cyberbullying and digital abuse are commonly seen in media reports across the globe highlighting the devastation caused to the family, friends and colleagues of a loved one unable to cope with their experience of bullying online. One of the most harmful facets of bullying online is the lack of respite that conventional bullying victims might experience when reaching the relative safety of their family home, with cyberbullying the problem follows; it follows wherever technology can reach. Simply not using technology isn't an option for most, especially for entire generations that have never experienced life without it, social media is an essential part of our social growth and development.

Golden rules

Don't respond

Cyberbullies want a reaction from you. That's why they do it.

Record

Keep a record of all evidence. You may need to show this to someone who can help.

Tell someone

Always tell someone. It could be a teacher, parent or trusted friend – don't suffer alone.

Say no to peer pressure

Don't get involved with sending, forwarding or liking cruel messages. If you're asked, just say no.

Stop and block

Block and report cyberbullies to your web site administrator.

⇨ The above information is reprinted with kind permission from CyberSmile. Please visit www.cybersmile.org for further information.

© CyberSmile 2016

Bullying campaigns

There have been many incidents of young people being driven to despair by bullying campaigns conducted through social media, with several suicides. Which comes closer to your view...

Bullying has always been rife among young people and this form is simply another channel – we shouldn't over-react	41%
We should treat this as a new kind of problem and create new laws and forms of policing to deal with it	53%
Not sure	5%

Do you think young people who engage in cyberbullying should be punished like criminals?

No	63%
Yes	21%
Not sure	16%

Source: Bullying campaigns, cyber-bullying, "forward air operating base", YouGov, 16 September 2015

Bullying and cyberbullying

Signs, symptoms and effects

It can be hard for adults, including parents, to know whether or not a child is being bullied. A child might not tell anyone because they're scared the bullying will get worse. They might think that they deserve to be bullied, or that it's their fault.

You can't always see the signs of bullying. And no one sign indicates for certain that a child's being bullied. But you should look out for:

⇨ belongings getting 'lost' or damaged

⇨ physical injuries such as unexplained bruises

⇨ being afraid to go to school, being mysteriously 'ill' each morning or skipping school

⇨ not doing as well at school

⇨ asking for, or stealing, money (to give to a bully)

⇨ being nervous, losing confidence or becoming distressed and withdrawn

⇨ problems with eating or sleeping

⇨ bullying others.

Things you may notice

If you're worried that a child is being abused, watch out for any unusual behaviour:

⇨ withdrawn

⇨ suddenly behaves differently

⇨ anxious

⇨ clingy

⇨ depressed

⇨ aggressive

⇨ problems sleeping

⇨ eating disorders

⇨ wets the bed

⇨ soils clothes

⇨ takes risks

⇨ misses school

⇨ changes in eating habits

⇨ obsessive behaviour

⇨ nightmares

⇨ drugs

⇨ alcohol

⇨ self-harm

⇨ thoughts about suicide.

The impact of bullying and cyberbullying

Bullying can have devastating effects which can last into adulthood. At its worst, bullying has driven children and young people to self-harm and even suicide.

All children who are affected by bullying can suffer harm – whether they are bullied, they bully others or they witness bullying.

Mental health problems

Children and young people who are bullied are more at risk of developing mental health problems, including depression and anxiety. Children at the highest risk are those who are both bullied, and who bully others (Victoria Department of Education and Early Childhood Development, 2013; NICHD, 2012).

Children who are bullied also:

⇨ have fewer friendships

⇨ aren't accepted by their peers

⇨ are wary and suspicious of others

⇨ have problems adjusting to school and don't do as well.

Effects on children who bully others

Children and young people who bully are at increased risk of:

⇨ substance misuse

⇨ academic problems

⇨ violent behaviour in later life.

Effects on children who witness bullying

Children who witness bullying may show similar signs as children who are being bullied. They may:

⇨ become reluctant to go to school

⇨ be frightened or unable to act

⇨ feel guilty for not doing anything to help.

References

⇨ National Institute of Child Health and Human Development (NICHD) (2012), *How does bullying affect health and wellbeing*. Bethesda, MD: National Institute of Child Health and Human Development (NICHD).

⇨ Victoria Department of Education and Early Childhood Development (2013), *The impact of bullying*. Melbourne: Department of Education and Early Childhood Development.

⇨ The above information is reprinted with kind permission from the NSPCC. Please visit www.nspcc.org.uk for further information.

Who is affected by bullying and cyberbullying?

Nearly all children will be affected by bullying in some way. They might be a victim of bullying, they might bully others, or they may witness bullying.

Even if they aren't directly affected, it's likely they'll know another child who is bullied or who bullies others.

Why bullying or cyberbullying happens

Any child can be bullied for any reason. If a child is seen as different in some way, or seen as an easy target they can be more at risk.

This might be because of their:

⇨ race

⇨ gender

⇨ sexual orientation.

Or it could be because they:

⇨ appear anxious or have low self-esteem

⇨ lack assertiveness

⇨ are shy or introverted.

Popular or successful children are also bullied, sometimes because others are jealous of them.

Sometimes a child's family circumstance or home life can be a reason for someone bullying them.

Disabled children can experience bullying because they seem an easy target and less able to defend themselves. 85% of parents of disabled children who had been bullied believed they were targeted because of their disability, according to one online survey.

Racist bullying

Racist bullying targets a child because of their:

⇨ skin colour

⇨ cultural or religious background

⇨ accent or the language they speak

⇨ ethnic origin.

25% of children from minority ethnic backgrounds had experienced racist bullying, according to one study carried out in mainly white schools.

Sexual bullying

Sexual bullying happens when gender or sexuality is used as a weapon by boys or girls towards others. Both boys and girls can suffer sexual bullying, but it's more common for girls to be victims.

Homophobic bullying

Homophobic bullying is the second most common form of bullying at school (after bullying because of weight). Young people may experience homophobic bullying if they're lesbian, gay, bisexual or transgender – or if others think they are. They might also be targeted because they have gay friends or family, or just because they're seen to be different.

55% of young people who identify as lesbian, gay or bisexual experienced homophobic bullying at school.

Why children bully others

There are many reasons why children bully others and it's not always straightforward. They might not even realise that what they're doing is bullying.

Peer pressure plays an important part in bullying among children and young people. Children may bully because they want the approval of others.

Children aren't always older or bigger than the child they're bullying – they might have some other advantage which makes them feel powerful. On the other hand, they might bully others because they feel powerless – perhaps because they've been a victim of bullying.

If a child has problems communicating, or difficulty with their behaviour, then they may lack social skills or find it hard to understand how others feel.

Sometimes children become aggressive or impulsive because they suffered harsh or inconsistent discipline, or lacked warmth and care, from their parents or carers.

Risk factors for all child abuse and neglect

There's still a lot we don't know about why abuse happens, but research has highlighted some similarities among children who have been abused or neglected. These similarities, or risk factors, help us identify children who may be at increased risk of abuse and neglect.

Some risk factors are common across all types of abuse and neglect. But they don't mean that abuse will definitely happen. A child who doesn't have any of these risk

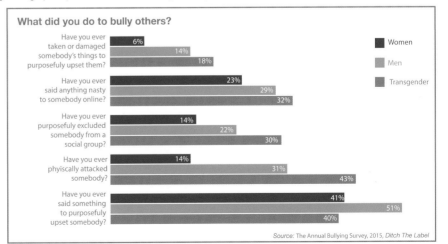

What did you do to bully others?

- Have you ever taken or damaged somebody's things to purposefully upset them? — Women 6%, Men 14%, Transgender 18%
- Have you ever said anything nasty to somebody online? — Women 23%, Men 29%, Transgender 32%
- Have you ever purposefuly excluded somebody from a social group? — Women 14%, Men 22%, Transgender 30%
- Have you ever phyiscally attacked somebody? — Women 14%, Men 31%, Transgender 43%
- Have you ever said something to purposefuly upset somebody? — Women 41%, Men 51%, Transgender 40%

Source: The Annual Bullying Survey, 2015, Ditch The Label

factors could be abused and a child with multiple risk factors may never experience abuse or neglect. But we do know that having one or more of these issues can increase the risk of harm.

Children who are at risk

Disabled children

Disabled children are over three times more likely to be abused or neglected than non-disabled children.

Some disabled children may not understand that what's happening to them is abuse and that it's wrong. Even if they do, they might not be able to ask for help. If a child is being abused by someone who looks after them or who they rely on to meet their needs it can be even harder for them to speak out or protect themselves.

Parents and professionals might mistake signs that a child is being abused or neglected as part of a child's impairment. And those working with disabled children may not be trained to spot the signs of abuse and neglect.

Children and families who feel isolated or without support due to a limited number of accessible services, may not know who to turn to to get help.

Parents who are abusive or neglectful might excuse their behaviour, blaming it on the difficulties of caring for a disabled child. Professionals focused on supporting parents to meet the needs relating to their child's disability may overlook parenting behaviours that are not good enough.

Professionals working in child protection might not have the specialised skills to accurately assess or understand a disabled child's needs, or to communicate with them properly.

Children in care

Most children who are in care live safely but a small number do experience harm. There are a number of risk factors related to being in care which can make children more vulnerable to abuse and neglect.

Children who have experienced other forms of abuse

Children who have been abused or neglected in the past are more likely to experience further abuse than children who haven't been abused or neglected. This is known as revictimisation.

Children who are being abused or neglected are also likely to be experiencing another form of abuse at the same time. This is known as polyvictimisation.

Children from black and mixed ethnic backgrounds

There don't appear to be links between ethnic groups and child abuse or neglect.

But children from black and mixed ethnic backgrounds are over-represented in the care system and in the children in need statistics. Children from Asian backgrounds are under-represented.

> **"Disabled children are over three times more likely to be abused or neglected than non-disabled children."**

This may be a result of a variety of issues including:

⇨ racial discrimination

⇨ language barriers

⇨ community and cultural norms and practices, such as female genital mutilation or harsh physical discipline

⇨ inadequate or inappropriate services

⇨ no action being taken for fear of upsetting cultural norms.

⇨ The above information is reprinted with kind permission from the NSPCC. Please visit www.nspcc.org.uk/bullying for further information.

Popular school students get bullied too

***An article from* The Conversation.**

By Ara Sarafian, Editor at The Conversation

Interviewed: Mark Rubin, Senior Lecturer in Social Psychology, University of Newcastle, Norman Feather, Emeritus Professor of Psychology, Flinders University, Robert Faris, Associate Professor of Sociology, University of California, Davis

The stereotype that popular kids don't get bullied has been busted by a new study that found becoming more popular at school can actually increase a student's risk of being bullied.

The study, published today in the *American Sociological Review*, surveyed more than 4,200 students from the 8th, 9th and 10th grades in 19 schools in North Carolina and examined how social status affects the risk of peer victimisation.

Popularity was determined by how central students were in their school's web of friendships. Bullying, or victimisation, was measured by analysing interviews in which students nominated up to five schoolmates who picked on them or were mean to them, and up to five peers whom they picked on or were mean to.

The study found the likelihood of victimisation increased by 25% when a typical student climbed to the top 5% of the social hierarchy.

Lead author and sociologist Robert Faris, from the University of California, found traditional patterns of bullying, such as on vulnerable kids who had few friends or poor body image.

"But we also found evidence of a second, counter-intuitive pattern where relatively popular kids are being targeted," he said.

It was only when students reached the very peak and were within the top 5% of the social hierarchy that their likelihood of being victimised dramatically decreased.

"The climb to the top of the social ladder is painful but the top rungs appear to offer a safe perch above the fray," Dr Faris said.

Social psychologist Norman Feather, from Flinders University, South Australia, said it might be because these high-status adolescents have more power and influence with the capacity to cause harm if attacked in some way.

"They may also be seen to be entitled to and deserve their high status," Professor Feather said.

The harder they fall

The study found that in rare cases when those at the very top do get victimised, the negative consequences are magnified.

High-status students experienced more depression, anxiety, anger and social marginalisation as result of a given incident of bullying.

The study said this could be because they had more to lose or perhaps because they were more unsuspecting victims.

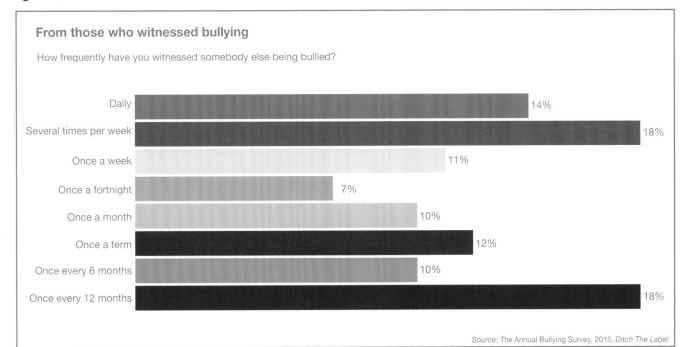

From those who witnessed bullying

How frequently have you witnessed somebody else being bullied?

Daily	14%
Several times per week	18%
Once a week	11%
Once a fortnight	7%
Once a month	10%
Once a term	12%
Once every 6 months	10%
Once every 12 months	18%

Source: The Annual Bullying Survey, 2015, *Ditch The Label*

Social psychologist Mark Rubin, from the University of Newcastle, New South Wales, said it was a case of "the bigger they are, the harder they fall".

"Although these highest-status children are less prone to victimisation, I wonder if they are nonetheless stressed out about the possibility of an attack on their high-status position," he said.

Tall poppy syndrome

This research relates to tall poppy syndrome, where people of genuine merit are resented or cut down because their achievements distinguish them from their peers.

Professor Feather's research showed that people who are low in status and self-esteem are more inclined to feel happier when tall poppies fall.

"It brings them closer to their own position," he said.

His research found that people are more accepting of tall poppies, and of other people with higher status, if they think the higher status was earned.

"People are less happy about the fall of a tall poppy if a tall poppy deserved their high position and did not deserve a fall from grace," he said.

But if the failure was deserved, people expressed pleasure and satisfaction at the misfortune.

Dr Rubin's research also showed that the need to be fair and equitable may influence people's behaviour towards others.

Out of school

These sorts of social psychological processes may not be limited to school environments.

"They are likely to occur within many social groups, including businesses, politics, even among scientists," Dr Rubin said.

"The need for social status may be driven by a more general motive for self-esteem.

"Most of us want to feel good about ourselves, and knowing that others value us provides an important means of establishing our self-esteem."

Professor Feather said it would be interesting to see if the results of this new American study replicate in Australia, where we emphasise equality as well as achievement.

"We need to protect the tall poppies who deserve their high status because they may do much to promote the advance of our society and culture," he said.

A new approach to bullying

Bullying intervention programmes often focus on addressing a lack in social skills in and empathy for those who are bullied. But Dr Faris said the new research showed that the competition for prestige was also a cause.

"To reduce bullying, it may be useful for schools to dedicate more attention and resources to de-emphasising social status hierarchies, perhaps by fostering a greater diversity of activities that promote a variety of interest-based friendship groups and not celebrating one activity – such as basketball or football – over any other."

1 April 2014

What is homophobic bullying?

Advice on LGBTQ bullying

Homophobic bullying is when people behave or speak in a way which makes someone feel bullied because of their actual or perceived sexuality. People may be a target of this type of bullying because of their appearance, behaviour, physical traits or because they have friends or family who are lesbian, gay, bisexual, transgender, or questioning or possibly just because they are seen as being different.

"Telling everyone in the dining hall, class, individuals, family at community events/ school events that I am gay (I am not gay), even going up to my parents telling them I am, and saying crude things, homophobic things, but I am not gay."

Like all forms of bullying, homophobic bullying can be through name calling, spreading rumours, cyberbullying, physical or sexual and emotional abuse. Young people have described to us how they have been subjected to hate campaigns against them which can start off within the classroom and then moved onto social media. This has devastated those being bullied in this way and some have moved schools and had their lives disrupted because of the actions of the bullies.

Not only does this affect a young person's self-esteem, emotional health and wellbeing but it also can have an effect on their attendance at school and their attainment. This type of bullying can also include threats to 'out' you to friends and family about your sexuality, even if you are not gay, lesbian or bisexual.

How common is it?

Homophobic bullying is the most frequent form of bullying after name calling. According to Stonewall's *School report*, 96% of gay pupils hear homophobic remarks such as 'poof' or 'lezza' used in school. 99% hear phrases such as 'that's so gay' or 'you're so gay' in school. 54%

of lesbian, gay and bisexual young people don't feel there is an adult at school who they can talk to about being gay. Worryingly, 6% of lesbian, gay and bisexual pupils are subjected to death threats.

**"I can't tell anyone because, basically, noone knows that I am gay... I got punched in the corridor today for example, and I can't tell the teacher because it will involve coming out."
Nick, 14 (via Stonewall)**

"It's important to remember that not everyone who experiences homophobic bullying is LGBT or questioning their sexuality," says Miriam Lynn, project support worker with the Cambridge-based charity SexYOUality. "It can happen to anyone."

Within our TeenBoundaries workshops at secondary schools working with young people, we explore homophobic bullying in more depth, looking at the journey of name calling, how it makes a person feel, the effects on their behaviour and what can happen as a result. A survey by the UK National Union of Teachers (NUT) shows that the most prevalent issue is sexual verbal abuse and being called obscene names. The names that cause most offence are homophobic terms. 65% of gay or bisexual young people experience homophobic bullying in school. 66% of LGBT young people suffer from bullying at school, 58% of them never report and half of them skip school as a result.

Tips on dealing with LGBTQ bullying

If you're being bullied in this way you need to tell your parents and report it to a teacher. Keep a diary of the remarks or behaviour. If you feel unable to speak to your parents or a teacher, perhaps you can approach another adult you can trust to get some help. Hopefully, if you have good friends, they can give you support to help get it stopped too.

If you feel able to, ignore the bullying so you are not giving the bully the reaction they are looking for. You can also be assertive and let them know that they are the ones that are looking stupid and ignorant. It is important to note, that if you feel they could get aggressive, then do not put yourself at risk as your safety is more important.

If this bullying spills over into threats or violence then it should be reported to the police as a hate crime. Many police forces have specialist units to deal with these incidents.

If you are being bullied online or via social media, take screenshots and keep them as evidence to show your parents, the school or the police.

Ask the school to do some work on LGBTQ bullying within your school if you feel able to; sometimes educating others can help enormously in making them realise their actions and consequences.

In many cases the people who are picking on you are projecting their prejudice on to others. They may also hear homophobic remarks being used by other people who hold outdated attitudes and think it is acceptable to act in this way when clearly it is not. This can often show their ignorance and closed minds.

What can parents do?

Parents and carers can play an important role in tackling homophobic bullying, says Stonewall's Chris Gibbons. He suggests:

⇨ Talk to your child. Ask how they are feeling and if everything is OK at school, rather than if they are being bullied. They may be embarrassed and worried that you will think they are gay, so might choose not to say anything.

⇨ Remember that homophobic bullying can affect any young person, regardless of their sexual orientation. Just because your child is experiencing homophobic bullying does not necessarily mean that he or she is lesbian, gay or bisexual.

Be supportive. Your child needs to know that if they do decide to talk to you about bullying, you will listen and that they can trust you with what they tell you. Let them tell you in their own time, and ask them how they want to proceed. Preferably approach the school together.

Check with the school what procedures they have in place for dealing with bullying and in particular, homophobic bullying. Involve your child in any decisions that are taken on how to tackle the bullying. If you are not satisfied with how your child's teacher responds, talk to the head teacher or bring it to the attention of the school governors – including your child at every stage.

Sue Allen of FFLAG (Family and Friends of Lesbians and Gays) advises that you check that the school has a separate anti-homophobic bullying policy and not something tacked on to their general bullying policy. Ask to see it, and if they haven't got one, ask why not and insist this is remedied. Go into the school and challenge them. They have a duty of care to all children. Research shows that in schools where children are explicitly taught that homophobic bullying is wrong, rates of such bullying are dramatically reduced, and pupils feel safer. Schools have a legal obligation to deal with homophobic bullying under the Education and Inspections Act 2006.

If the bullying doesn't stop, go to your Local Education Authority and demand action. Changing schools can work in some cases but often a vulnerable child is vulnerable wherever they go. Encourage your child to take up judo or another form of self-defence. This will boost their confidence that they can defend themselves if necessary.

What should schools do about homophobic bullying?

Schools should deal with homophobic bullying by including it in their bullying policies. According to Stonewall's *Teachers' Report 2014* survey, Nine in ten secondary school teachers say students in their schools are bullied, harassed or called names for being, or perceived to be, lesbian, gay or bi. Yet nine in ten primary and secondary school staff have never received any specific training on how to prevent and respond to this type of bullying. Stonewall has lots of educational resources for schools and teachers from free DVDs to classroom resources.

Some schools are also dealing with this by raising it in citizenship lessons, looking at how to tackle prejudice and discrimination. There are a number of organisations which help pupils with these issues, including Stonewall, Diversity Role Models and Schools Out.

The above information is reprinted with kind permission from Family Lives. Please visit www.bullying.co.uk for further information.

Bullying myths and facts

There are many myths surrounding bullying issues and some of these myths can often trivialise bullying and suggest the bullied individual is making a big deal out of nothing when actually that is not the case. This can undermine how a person feels if they are being bullied. Bullying should not be tolerated in any form. We believe it is important to address bullying whether it is in a workplace, school or in a neighbourhood so that the message is clear that bullying is unacceptable.

The myths and facts below can be a great discussion point to raise awareness of bullying with children and young people.

Myth: Bullying is a normal part of childhood and you should just ignore it

Fact: Bullying is not 'normal' or acceptable in any form and ignoring might not always make it stop. If you can, please confide in someone you trust such as a parent or teacher to help you get it stopped. Bullying can knock your self-esteem and confidence.

Myth: It is OK to hit someone who is bullying you, it will stop it

Fact: It's understandable that you may be angry but if you were to get violent or aggressive it may make matters much worse as you may get into trouble too.

Myth: Bullies are born this way, it's in their genes

Fact: Bullies often adopt this behaviour from their environment or, sometimes, it's a reaction from them being bullied by others. Whatever the case, it is not right.

Myth: Bullying only happens in schools

Fact: This is not the case at all, bullying can happen to anyone at any place. It may be out of school, at university or even college. It can happen when you are out with mates or on the way to or from school.

Myth: You can spot a bully from the way they look and act

Fact: There is no such thing as a way a bully looks or acts. There is no specific dress code or behaviour code.

Myth: Online bullying is just banter and harmless

Fact: People being bullied online is a very serious issue, the bullying can go viral very quickly and make the problem escalate quickly. It is important to take a screenshot of any conversations, messages or posts that you feel are bullying so that you have a record.

Myth: Cyberbullying doesn't involve physical harm so what's the harm?

Fact: Actually, some people have committed suicide as a result of not seeing any way out of the non-stop harassment, threats and abuses. The emotional scarring stays for a lot longer and sometimes a person will never get over this. Some websites allow people to post anonymously, which can mean it is very hard to stop this abuse.

Myth: Cyberbullying can only affect someone if they are online and have an account too

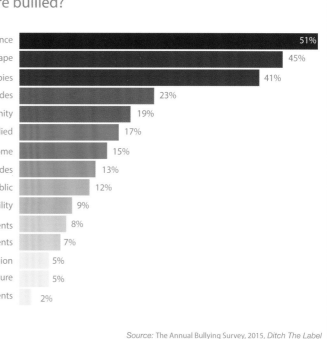

Why do you think you were bullied?

Attitudes towards appearance	51%
Attitudes towards weight/body shape	45%
Attitudes towards my interests/hobbies	41%
Attitudes towards my high grades	23%
Attitudes towards levels of masculinity	19%
Because a family member or friend is also bullied	17%
Attitudes towards household income	15%
Attitudes towards my low grades	13%
Attitudes towards a family issue made public	12%
Attitudes towards my disability	9%
Racist bullying and comments	8%
Homohate bullying and comments	7%
Attitudes towards my religion	5%
Attitudes towards my culture	5%
Transhate bullying and comments	2%

Source: The Annual Bullying Survey, 2015, *Ditch The Label*

Fact: This is not true, we often hear of pages and fake accounts being created without a person's permission or knowledge. This sort of cyberbullying is on the increase and just as serious as any other form of bullying.

Myth: It is not bullying if someone deletes the comment or post

Fact: Regardless of hitting delete, once something is posted online it gets its own unique URL which means that it can stay on cyberspace even if you hit delete.

Myth: If bullying was so bad, why don't they have a law about it?

Fact: Some forms of bullying are illegal and should be reported to the police, including violence or assault, theft, repeated harassment or intimidation, e.g. threats and abusive phone calls, e-mails or text messages and hate crimes.

Myth: Reporting a bully will make things worse

Fact: You may worry that reporting a bully might make the bullying escalate or feel you are not believed. It is important to confide in someone you trust so that you can have some help in getting the necessary support to get this stopped.

Myth: It is easy to spot the signs of bullying

Fact: It is not always easy to spot the signs of bullying as it is not always physical and obvious. Emotional, verbal and online bullying can often leave scars that people don't see.

Myth: Children grow out of bullying

Fact: Quite often children who bully may grow up to be adults who bully or use negative behaviour to get what they want, unless there has been intervention and their behaviour challenged by the relevant authorities, whether it be school or parents, etc.

⇨ The above information is reprinted with kind permission from Family Lives. Please visit www.bullying.co.uk for further information.

BYE!

Who are more likely to be bullies – poor kids or rich kids?

An article from **The Conversation.**

THE CONVERSATION

By Neil Tippett, PhD Student, University of Warwick, Dieter Wolke and Professor of Psychology, University of Warwick

Bullying is the repeated and systematic abuse of power with the aim of causing intentional harm. Examples of bullying have been found in all societies, including among modern hunter-gatherers and in ancient civilisations. But new research has shown that in the modern age, we can draw few strong conclusions about whether bullies are more likely to come from richer or poorer families. In hierarchical social settings, anybody can be at risk of bullying.

Some researchers consider bullying to be an evolutionary adaptation, designed to gain access to resources, secure survival, and allow for more mating opportunities. Bullying can also reduce stress upon bullies: by enabling them to develop a culture of fear and respect, it deters others from attacking them and means they have to spend less of their time fighting.

While children diagnosed with conduct disorder or delinquency are more often found in socially disadvantaged groups, such as among families with low socioeconomic status, it is less clear whether bullies are also more likely to come from these backgrounds.

If bullies are motivated by the desire to obtain greater status and dominance, and use strategic behaviour as a means of gaining social success and romantic partners, then it is likely they will be found in similar numbers among all socioeconomic groups.

Richer or poorer?

To explore this, we investigated whether being a victim, bully or bully/victim (someone who is victim but also fights back) was associated with socioeconomic status. Our research synthesised findings from 28 studies published since 1970 covering 342,611 children and adolescents in North America, Europe and Australia.

We found a weak association between socioeconomic status and being a bully: bullies were only slightly more likely to come from middle or lower socioeconomic backgrounds. In contrast, victims and bully/victims were more likely to live in poorer families. Fewer victims came from richer households.

The results suggest that bullies exist across all socioeconomic groups: they are as likely to be found in deprived inner city areas as they are in leafy, suburban schools in well-to-do neighbourhoods. In contrast, those who become victims, particularly victims who retaliate unsuccessfully (bully/victims), are more likely to be raised in less well-off families. Overall, it seems that socioeconomic status is not the most accurate indicator for identifying those involved in school bullying.

A social strategy

These findings for bullies support an evolutionary interpretation of bullying situations. Unlike other forms of child aggression, such as conduct disorder or delinquency, which can result from psychiatric problems within the child, bullying appears to be a social strategy, which is used to gain access to resources and achieve greater social status.

Emerging evidence shows that bullies are more prevalent in social settings characterised by hierarchical social structures, and more financial or social inequality. Greater financial inequality in nations, as well as more hierarchical classroom and household structures all increase the risk of children bullying others. The more unequal a social setting, the more likely it is that using any means of getting ahead is endorsed.

Contrary to views held by some teachers, parents and even psychiatrists that bullies are poorly adjusted, there is also increasing evidence that bullies excel at reading other people's emotions, and are often skilled manipulators who use a variety of social strategies. These may range from classical bullying (verbal, physical, blackmailing or social exclusion) to more 'pro-social strategies' such as publicly offering favours that make the victim feel uncomfortable and cannot be repaid.

The benefits to bullies have recently been shown in a range of longitudinal studies, which found bullying others had few psychological, health or economic downsides in early adulthood. It has actually been shown that being a bully may be protective for health: bullies were found to have less 'chronic

inflammation' – caused when the body tries to fight an infectious agent – and therefore might be at a decreased risk for developing cardiovascular or metabolic illness.

Reasons for being picked on

In contrast, low socioeconomic status does somewhat increase the risk of being victimised at school. Standing out from the rest of the peer group such as being unable to afford lifestyle items may single out children for victimisation.

Alternatively, characteristics which differ by socioeconomic level, such as parenting strategies, may explain this association. Harsh parenting practices and greater rates of domestic violence increase the risk of being victims or bully/victims, but are also more often found in low socioeconomic households. Overprotective, or so-called 'helicopter parenting', in particular, increases the risk of becoming a victim of bullying.

Overall, bullies are found in all socioeconomic groups while victims or bully/victims are slightly more likely to come from lower socioeconomic backgrounds. To predict who might become a victim or bully/victim, a combination of background, family factors such as parenting or sibling relationships, and individual characteristics need to be considered.

As bullies are found in all social strata, social conditions can mean that anyone is at risk of becoming a victim, particularly those in hierarchical school settings who are new or different, and have few friends to support them.

22 July 2014

⇨ The above information is reprinted with kind permission from *The Conversation*. Please visit www.theconversation.com for further information.

Girl bullies "could be great leaders", says expert

"Mean girls" who rule the playground through fear should be matched with positive role models to make the best of their leadership skills, says an expert.

By Javier Espinoza and Elizabeth Roberts

From Queen Elizabeth I – famous for her fiery temper – to Margaret Thatcher and her habit of 'handbagging' those who annoyed her, many great leaders have had a tendency towards bullying behaviour.

And now, a chartered psychologist has suggested that girls who bully their classmates at school and leave playmates quaking in their boots should be seen as great female leaders of the future.

Suggesting the young tyrants should be supported by adults, rather than just punished, Dr Sam Littlemore told the *Sunday Telegraph* that "alpha females" tend to manipulate those around them through fear.

However, they can learn how to be nice but effective through teaming them up with kinder leaders, who can help them use their power in a less anti-social way.

"Allow her to spend time with another girl who is the head of a group who helps with parents' evenings. Let the girl bully associate herself not necessarily with a good girl but a girl who has strong leadership skills," said Dr Littlemore, who has advised thousands of schools on the issue.

This way, the girl will learn that she can "still be strong and influence people and that she can do it in a kinder way without getting into trouble all the time".

Dr Littlemore, the author of *Girl Bullying: Do I Look Bothered?* also said these "alpha females" should be exposed to bullying behaviour through fictional characters like Regina George from the film *Mean Girls* to help them understand that their behaviour is unhelpful.

She said: "Show her a story where there has been bullying and ask her for the characteristics of that behaviour.

This is like a mirror but it's not asking her to look at herself directly because that can be scary for many people."

The expert said that by doing so the girl will understand "that she can change her behaviour and that she has choice".

Writing in *Teach Primary* magazine, she explained the psychology behind a girl bully. She wrote: "She gathers her pack, those who are happy to follow and graze in her shadow, as she is desperate to establish and maintain a role at the top of the social hierarchy. She controls them with fear and threats. She destroys her victims to show her power.

"And why? Because she can. Because adults around her dismiss the pack behaviour as just 'girls being girls' and the children learn that it must be OK for her to rule because no one challenges her."

However, she said such children are often terrified inside, and feeling lost.

Dr Littlemore emphasised, however, that while bullying girls should be given support from adults, "sanctions" should also take part to deter their behaviour.

Her comments follow research that showed two in three girls say they are being bullied, with girls more likely to fall victims of cruelty.

16 January 2016

⇨ The above information is reprinted with kind permission from *The Telegraph*. Please visit www.telegraph.co.uk for further information.

The effects of bullying

Although there are three main groups that are affected by bullying – the students who are bullied, the students who bully and the bystanders who see it happen, bullying encompasses and affects the entire school community, families and friendship groups.

Bullying creates a culture of fear and has a negative impact on everyone involved. Being bullied can seriously affect a person's physical, emotional, academic and social wellbeing. Many sufferers of bullying lack confidence, feel bad about themselves, have few friends and spend a lot of time alone.

Bullying is a very stressful ordeal, one that many people find it hard to speak about. Those being bullied continually ask why me? They may feel ashamed and embarrassed that they are not standing up to the bully and deal with what is happening to them.

Bullying can have devastating effects on a person which can last into adulthood. At its worst, bullying has driven children and young people to self-harm and even suicide.

Effect of bullying on the bullied

Those who are bullied may:

⇨ Feel disconnected from school and not want to attend

⇨ Have lower academic outcomes, including lower attendance

⇨ Lack quality friendships at school

⇨ Display high levels of emotion that indicate vulnerability and low levels of resilience

⇨ Avoid conflict and be socially withdrawn

⇨ Have low self-esteem

⇨ Become depressed, anxious and lonely

⇨ Have nightmares

⇨ Feel wary or suspicious of others

⇨ In extreme cases, have a higher risk of self-harm and/or suicide.

Effect of bullying on bullies

People who frequently bully others may:

⇨ Display high levels of aggressive behaviour which can impact on their future

⇨ Struggle to develop and maintain effective relationships

⇨ Have difficulty integrating into the workplace

⇨ Have low self-esteem

⇨ Have difficulty understanding boundaries and limits.

Effect of bullying on bystanders

Those who witness bullying may:

⇨ Be reluctant to attend school

⇨ Feel fearful, scared and guilty for not doing anything

⇨ Experience pressure to participate in the bullying

⇨ Become anxious and worried.

⇨ The above information is reprinted with kind permission from BulliesOut. Please visit www.bulliesout.com for further information.

© BulliesOut 2016

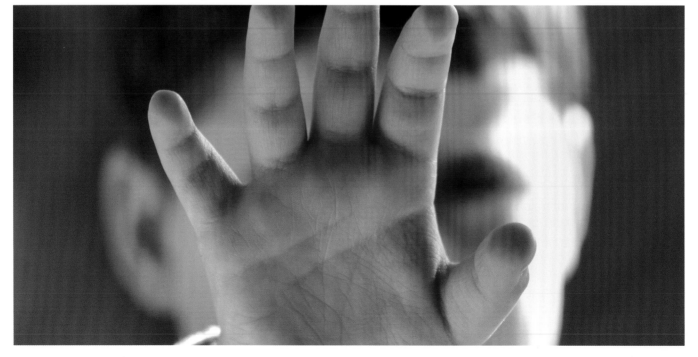

Focus on: Bullying and Mental Health

An extract from the report by the Anti-Bullying Alliance and the National Children's Bureau.

What is mental health?

Mental health is an integral part of who we are. It governs how we are able to think, feel and behave, and maintaining good mental health is as important to our wellbeing as having good physical health. Despite the negative connotations and stigma attached to them, mental health problems are common, with up to one in four people in the UK experiencing mental health problems each year.[1] There are many different mental health problems, but some of the most common include:

⇨ Depression

⇨ Anxiety disorders

⇨ Schizophrenia

⇨ Bipolar disorder

⇨ Personality disorders

⇨ Eating disorders.

Although not defined as mental health problems themselves, there are also specific feelings or behaviours, such as self-harming and suicidal thoughts, which are closely associated with, and in some cases brought about by, other mental health problems. As with any physical illness, mental health problems can pose significant life challenges, but can be recovered from with the appropriate help and support, such that many people who have experienced mental health problems are able to go on and lead productive, fulfilling lives.

The impact of bullying on mental health

The links between school bullying and mental health have been known for a long time.[2] Some of the earliest studies of school bullying showed how being bullied could lead to children feeling sad, withdrawn and anxious, all of which are key indicators of mental health problems. As research in this area has continued to grow, it has become clear that the experience of being bullied, and in some cases bullying others, can have a negative impact on all aspects of a child's mental functioning.[2]

Are mental health problems a cause or consequence of bullying?

Before discussing this research, one key factor that must be taken into account is the direction of causality: does bullying lead to mental health problems, or are children with existing mental health problems more likely to be involved in bullying? Research shows that many of the symptoms associated with mental health problems, such as behavioural or emotional difficulties, act as significant risk factors for bullying involvement.[3] Children who have low self-esteem, are anxious or socially withdrawn, and who have behavioural, emotional or peer relationship problems are at greater risk of becoming victims or bully-victims at school. Additionally, children who exhibit behavioural difficulties and conduct problems may be more likely to engage in bullying others.[3] While many of these characteristics may be present before children become involved in school bullying, there is also evidence that bullying can exacerbate these problems further, such that someone who is bullied because they are anxious and socially withdrawn, becomes further isolated and worried as a result of being bullied.[4] The association between bullying and mental health represents a vicious circle, where children who are already vulnerable and at risk suffer further at the hands of their peers, thus worsening their outcomes, and the likelihood of experiencing more severe mental health issues.

Distinguishing between mental health problems that are preexisting and those that arise solely as a result of bullying is a focus of current research, and one that helps us to determine the true damage that bullying can cause. Contemporary studies have begun to use longitudinal data, which is comparable data gathered over a specific period of time, to show the independent effect that bullying has upon mental health outcomes. After controlling for external influences which may affect mental health, such as family history or household situation, longitudinal studies are now able to compare how children perform on mental health variables both before and after incidents of bullying, thereby showing the unique contribution that bullying has had towards a person's mental health.

November 2015

⇨ The above information is reprinted with kind permission from the National Children's Bureau. Please visit www.anti-bullyingalliance.org.uk for further information.

1   MIND. *What are mental health problems?* [13/11/15]; Available from: http://www.mind.org.uk/.

2   Arseneault, L., L. Bowes, and S. Shakoor, *Bullying victimization in youths and mental health problems: "Much ado about nothing"?*, Psychological Medicine, 2010. 40(5): p. 717-729

3   Wolke, D., S.T. Lereya, and N. Tippett, *Individual and social determinants of bullying and cyberbullying*, in Cyberbullying and youth: From theory to interventions, T. Vollink, F. Dehue, and C. McGuckin, Editors. 2015, Psychology Press: New York.

4   Reijntjes, A., et al., *Peer victimization and internalizing problems in children: A meta-analysis of longitudinal studies.* Child Abuse & Neglect, 2010. 34(4): p. 244-252.

Bully victims more likely to suffer night terrors and nightmares

Children who are bullied at ages eight to ten are more likely to suffer from sleep walking, night terrors or nightmares by the time they are 12 years old.

In a study published this week in *Pediatrics*, journal of the American Pediatric Association, Professor Dieter Wolke and Dr Suzet Tanya Lereya from the University of Warwick, found being bullied increases the risk for a category of sleep disorders known as parasomnias. These are sleep-related problems such as nightmares, night terrors or sleepwalking.

A cohort of children from the Avon Longitudinal Study of Parents and Children (ALSPAC) were interviewed at elementary school age (eight and ten years) about bullying experiences and then about parasomnias at secondary school age (12–13 years).

Professor Wolke, from Warwick Medical School and the Department of Psychology, said: "We found children who were bullied at age eight or ten years were more likely to have nightmares, night terrors or sleepwalking at age 12 years. Moreover, those who were bullied and bullied others (bully/victims) were most likely to have any parasomnia.

"Consistent with previous studies, being a female, having persistent sleep problems, and emotional and behaviour problems in childhood additionally increased the risk for parasomnias at age 12 years."

Dr Lereya, from the Department of Psychology, added that stress could be an important mechanism for the association between being bullied and parasomnias.

Types of bullying	All young people who were bullied
I have been picked on verbally/emotionally abused	94%
I have been physically attacked	23%
I have been abused online/ cyberbullied	13%

Source: The Prince's Trust Youth Index 2015

"Nightmares may occur when anxiety exceeds a threshold level and several studies have suggested that trait anxiety may be related to the frequency of parasomnias. However, even after controlling for pre-existing anxiety problems our results showed that being bullied may increase the risk for parasomnias."

The authors suggest that: "If a child is experiencing frequent parasomnias, parents, teachers, school counsellors and clinicians may consider asking about bullying. This would allow detecting bullied children and providing the help they need at an early time to reduce the negative effects of being bullied."

11 September 2014

⇨ The above information is reprinted with kind permission from the University of Warwick. Please visit www2.warwick.ac.uk for further information.

Bullying may have worse long-term effects than child abuse

"Bullied children are five times more at risk of anxiety than those maltreated," reports the Daily Mail. A study looking at both UK and US children found an association between childhood bullying and anxiety, depression and self-harm in adulthood.

People bullied by their peers in childhood were found to be more likely to have mental health problems in young adulthood than those who were ill-treated by adults, including their parents.

But the headlines are misleading – this figure only reflects the results of the US study. The results from the UK part of the study, which included more than three times the number of children, were not nearly as dramatic.

There are also some problems with the way this study was designed. It relied on children and parents self-reporting their experiences, which may make the results less reliable. For obvious reasons, parents in particular may have played down their ill-treatment of their children.

Still, the authors' conclusion that schools, health services and other agencies should co-ordinate their response to bullying seems a valid suggestion.

If you are concerned that your child is being bullied, it's essential that you or your child, or both of you, talk to their school. You could ask to see their anti-bullying policy, which every school has to have by law. This will allow you to see how the school plans to prevent and tackle bullying.

Where did the story come from?

The study was carried out by researchers from the University of Warwick and Duke Medical Centre, both in the UK.

It was funded by The Wellcome Trust, the Medical Research Council, the Economic and Social Research Council in the UK, the National Institute of Mental Health, the National Institute on Drug Abuse, NARSAD (Early Career Award) and the William T Grant Foundation in the US.

It was published in the peer-reviewed medical journal, *The Lancet Psychiatry* on an open-access basis, so it is free to read online or download as a PDF.

The study was widely covered by the media. However, the *Mail's* assertion that bullied children are five times more at risk of anxiety than those maltreated by adults is misleading.

This figure was also used in other news sources and in an accompanying press release, but it only reflects the results of a US study. The figures from the UK, which involved more than three times the number of children, were not as striking.

What kind of research was this?

This was a cohort study exploring the long-term mental health effects of bullying in childhood compared with a child's ill-treatment by adults.

The researchers say ill-treatment by adults in childhood, such as neglect, cruelty and sexual abuse, is a matter of intense public concern. It has been shown to increase the risk of mental ill health, substance abuse and suicide attempts.

Verbal and physical abuse (bullying) by other children is also a global issue, with one in three children across 38 countries reporting being bullied. It can also have similar adverse effects in adulthood.

The researchers aimed to find out whether mental ill health is a result of both ill-treatment and bullying, or whether bullying has an independent effect.

What did the research involve?

The research was based on two large ongoing cohort studies of families. One involved 4,026 children from the UK and the other had 1,420 children from the US.

The UK study aims to look at the health and development of children during childhood and beyond. The participants were pregnant women with an expected delivery date between April 1991 and December 1992.

From the first term of pregnancy, parents in the study completed postal questionnaires about themselves and their child's health and development.

The mother provided information on maltreatment between the ages of eight weeks and 8.6 years, and their child's reports of bullying when they were aged eight, ten and 13. The term "maltreatment" was assessed as physical, emotional or sexual abuse, or "severe maladaptive parenting".

Children attended annual assessment clinics, including face-to-face interviews and psychological and physical tests, from the age of seven onwards.

The US study is based on a sample of three groups of children aged nine, 11 and 13 years who were recruited in 1993. The parents and children were repeatedly interviewed and asked about bullying and maltreatment.

This included any physical or sexual abuse, or harsh parental discipline. The children were screened for behavioural problems and mental disorders up until young adulthood.

The researchers controlled the results for factors thought to increase the risk of child abuse and bullying, including the sex of the child, family hardship and the mother's mental health. They assessed for these factors during pregnancy for the UK cohort, and at annual parent and child interviews for the US cohort.

What were the basic results?

The researchers found that:

⇨ In the US cohort, children who were bullied were nearly five times more likely to suffer anxiety than children who were maltreated (US cohort odds ratio [OR] 4.9; 95% confidence interval [CI] 2.0 to 12.0).

⇨ In the UK group, compared with children who were maltreated, children who were bullied were more likely to have depression (OR 1.7, 1.1–2.7) and self-harm (OR 1.7, 1.1–2.6).

⇨ In the US cohort, children who were maltreated but not bullied were four times more likely to have depression in young adulthood compared with children who were not maltreated or bullied (OR 4.1, 95% CI 1.5–11.7).

⇨ In the UK cohort, those who were maltreated but not bullied were not at an increased risk for any mental health problem compared with children who were not maltreated or bullied.

⇨ In both cohorts, those who were both maltreated and bullied were at an increased risk for overall mental health problems, anxiety and depression compared with children who were not maltreated or bullied. In the UK cohort, they were also at risk of self-harm.

⇨ In both cohorts, children who were bullied by peers but not ill-treated by adults were more likely to have mental health problems than children who were maltreated but not bullied (UK cohort 1.6, 95% CI 1.1–2.2; US cohort 3.8, 95% CI 1.8–7.9).

How did the researchers interpret the results?

The researchers say that being bullied by peers in childhood had generally worse long-term adverse effects on young adults' mental health than ill-treatment by adults.

The findings have important implications for public health planning and service development for dealing with peer bullying, they argue.

Conclusion

The two sets of results from differing cohort groups make the findings of this study quite confusing. For example, the abstract and press release highlight the 4.9% increase in anxiety when children had been bullied only, compared with children ill-treated by adults. But this figure only comes from the US cohort.

The confidence interval for this figure is very wide, suggesting it may not be reliable. In the UK cohort, the increased risk for anxiety among those who were bullied was small, but this was not included in the abstract or the press release.

The study relied on both adults and children self-reporting bullying or maltreatment by adults, which may undermine its reliability. Adults especially may be less inclined to report ill-treatment by themselves or a partner, although the authors tried to design the study in a way to guard against this. Also, as the authors point out, the study makes no distinction between abuse by adults and harsh parenting.

In the UK cohort, not all children completed the mental health assessment at 18 years. Those with more family problems were more likely to drop out, which could also make the results less reliable. There may also have been some selection bias of those people who agreed to participate in the study in the first place.

The study also failed to take cyberbullying into account, although the authors say previous studies have shown an overlap between "traditional" forms of bullying and cyberbullying.

Across both cohorts, about 40% of children who were ever maltreated were also bullied. As the authors point out, it is possible that being ill-treated may make children more susceptible to being bullied, or that both types of abuse have common risk factors.

29 April 2015

⇨ The above information is reprinted with kind permission from NHS Choices. Please visit www.nhs.uk for further information.

Nearly a third of early adulthood depression linked to bullying in teenage years

Bullying in teenage years is strongly associated with depression later on in life, suggests new research on Children of the 90s data published in **The BMJ** *this week.*

Depression is a major public health problem with high economic and societal costs. There is a rapid increase in depression from childhood to adulthood and one contributing factor could be bullying by peers. But the link between bullying at school and depression in adulthood is still unclear due to limitations in previous research.

So a team of scientists, led by Lucy Bowes at the University of Oxford, carried out one of the largest studies on the association between bullying by peers in teenage years and depression in early adulthood.

They undertook a longitudinal observational study that examined the relationship between bullying at 13 years and depression at 18 years.

They analysed bullying and depression data on 3,898 participants in the Avon Longitudinal Study of Parents and Children (ALSPAC), a UK community-based birth cohort popularly known as Children of the 90s.

The participants completed a self-report questionnaire at 13 years about bullying and at 18 years completed an assessment that identified individuals who met internationally agreed criteria for depressive illness.

Of the 683 teenagers who reported frequent bullying more than once a week at 13 years, 14.8% were depressed at 18 years. And of the 1,446 teenagers who had some bullying one to three times over six months at 13 years, 7.1% were depressed at 18 years.

Only 5.5% of teenagers who did not experience bullying were depressed at 18 years.

Around 10.1% of frequently bullied teenagers experienced depression for more than two years, compared with 4.1% from the non-bullied group.

Overall, 2,668 participants had data on bullying and depression as well as other factors that may have caused depression such as previous bullying in childhood, mental and behavioural problems, family set-up and stressful life events.

When these factors were taken into account, frequently bullied teenagers still had around a twofold increase in odds of depression compared with those who did not experience bullying. This association was the same for both males and females.

The most common type of bullying was name calling – 36% experienced this, while 23% had belongings taken.

Most teenagers never told a teacher (41%–74%) or a parent (24%–51%), but up to 75% told an adult about physical bullying such as being hit or beaten up.

If this were a causal relationship, up to 30% of depression in early adulthood could be attributable to bullying in teenage years, explain the authors, adding that bullying could make a substantial contribution to the overall burden of depression.

While this is an observational study and no definitive conclusions can be drawn about cause and effect, they say that interventions to reduce bullying in schools could reduce depression in later life.

In an accompanying editorial, Maria M Ttofi from the University of Cambridge writes that this study has clear anti-bullying messages that should be endorsed by parents, schools and practitioners. She also calls for more research to establish the causal links between bullying and depression, and to drive specific interventions to reduce victimisation.

2 June 2015

⇨ The above information is reprinted with kind permission from the University of Bristol. Please visit www.bristol.ac.uk for further information.

Find out if you are a bully

Have a look at the list below and answer the questions honestly.

Have you ever

⇨ Repeatedly called someone names?

⇨ Physically hurt someone on purpose (hitting, kicking, punching, etc.)?

⇨ Used your size to intimidate or threaten others?

⇨ Made fun of people you perceive as different?

⇨ Made fun of a person's culture or religion?

⇨ Laughed at someone because they have a disability?

⇨ Said nasty things about another person's weight, hair colour, skin colour or clothes?

⇨ Made fun of a person's sexuality?

⇨ Taken someone else's belongings?

⇨ Damaged or destroyed someone else's property?

⇨ Spread rumours about someone?

⇨ Said nasty things about someone behind their back?

⇨ Excluded someone from your group on purpose?

⇨ Sent someone nasty or threatening e-mails or texts?

⇨ Posted nasty comments about another person on a social networking site (Twitter, Facebook, etc.)?

⇨ Laughed at someone who is being picked on?

If you have answered yes to any of the above questions, then you are guilty of being a bully. Think about why you do these things. Is it because someone does it to you, or has done in the past and you're angry about that? Do you make someone else look small so you can feel better about yourself? Or are you scared that if you're not the bully, you may be the one getting bullied?

Some other reasons why you bully others may be listed below:

⇨ Are you jealous of the person you are bullying?

⇨ Worried about something that may be happening in your own life?

⇨ Being mistreated by someone in your life?

⇨ Are you hanging around with other bullies and want to fit in?

⇨ Do you like the feeling of power bullying gives you?

⇨ Do you think bullying someone makes you popular?

Have a good think to try and work out what makes you behave like this – then work to solve that problem. You'll feel much better if you deal with your issues rather than taking it out on someone else and you will ultimately be a much nicer person to be around.

Research has shown that by the age of 24, bullies are 60% more likely to have a criminal record than any other group (as quoted by Andy Tomko, *You Big Bully*, 2005). Surely this is not the sort of life you want for yourself?

⇨ The above information is reprinted with kind permission from BulliesOut. Please visit www.bulliesout.com for further information.

Why bullies don't feel bad (or don't know they do)

Bullies are unaware of their negative self-perceptions.

By Mary C Lamia Ph.D.

Advertising campaigns are promoting the idea that bullies truly feel bad about themselves. In one of the ads, for example, a girl denigrates others at school then disparages herself while viewing her own image in a locker mirror. Generally speaking, that's not how bullies operate. If you assume bullies are aware of feeling bad about themselves, you may be ineffective in dealing with them. Attacking others actually enables bullies to be unaware of what they really feel. Thus, you probably won't find a bully belittling her reflection in a mirror.

Bullies induce shame and humiliation in others by intuitively recognising a person's insecurities and attacking them. The bully's attacks are projections of their own shame and feelings of inadequacy that are modified to penetrate a victim's vulnerability. Attacking others not only halts any inclination to look within themselves, it also can be exciting as it stimulates the physical experience of power.[1] Although bullies diminish others in order to raise themselves up, they are not conscious of how negatively they feel about themselves. Diminishing others keeps their need to elevate themselves out of their conscious awareness.

Feeling sorry for bullies can make you ill equipped to handle them and yourself with them. A sympathetic response assumes the bully is aware of having a negative self-perception. Forgive the analogy, but imagine that a bully is like a frightened animal whose adaptation to experiencing fear early in life (like the bully's early responses to shame) automatically leads it to aggressively attack. Compassion is safe to feel if you are socialising the animal in a controlled environment. If instead you just happen to encounter it when you are alone and unsuspecting, you may be threatened or bitten.

As humans adapt to situations and circumstances in early life they develop a pattern of how they respond to shame. Distinctive shame responses colour the relationships we have with others and ourselves. These learned responses to feeling shame include withdrawal, avoidance, attacking oneself and attacking others.[2] In response to shame, withdrawal hides one's feelings from others and it can lead to isolated depression. This response is common in loneliness. An avoidance response implies a self-centred protectiveness that may involve the abuse of alcohol, substances or addictive behaviour. Another response to shame, attacking oneself in a psychologically or physically self-injurious way, is an acquiescent response. Self-blame can maintain a relationship, but it will be at the expense of keeping oneself a victim. Those who bully use the most primitive and destructive shame response: they attack others. The attack other response to shame occurs when an individual feels psychologically endangered and incompetent, and the family system in which the person has grown up has permitted the use of attack as a response.[3]

The notion that people bully others because they have low self-esteem implies they are aware of feeling bad about themselves as depicted in the ad campaign. If you accept the idea that bullies have low self-esteem, then it is essential to recognise they don't feel its impact, as you would normally expect. In a previous post I mentioned research demonstrating that bullies actually do not experience low self-esteem.[4] Instead their hubristic pride completely shields them from self-denigration. Hubris is related to egotism and, in some cases, to full blown maladaptive narcissism.

Bullies don't attack confident people. They attack what appears to them as weakness. Children and adults are vulnerable if they sympathise with bullies and believe they actually suffer from feeling the effects of low self-esteem. Further, victims of bullying tend to be sensitive people who are likely to attack themselves in response to being attacked. Children who unite in outrage against bullying will have a container for their feelings, since often victims of bullies are isolated or silent as a result of being shamed. In turn, by uniting, they contain the bully who faces the threat of isolation.

Perhaps the ad campaign against bullying should instead feature a bully who denigrates others, and then, upon seeing her own image in the locker mirror, sneers proudly at herself. Such a scenario would be closer to reality.

(For information about my publications, please visit my website: www.marylamia.com)

References
1. Nathanson, D. (1992). *Shame and Pride: Affect, Sex, and the Birth of the Self.* New York: Norton.
2. Nathanson, D. (1992), cited above.
3. Nathanson, D. (1992), cited above.
4. Thomaes, S., Bushman, B. J., Stegge, H., & Olthof, T. (2008). *Trumping shame by blasts of noise: Narcissism, self-esteem, shame, and aggression in young adolescents.* Child Development, 79, 1792-1801.

1 March 2015

⇨ The above information is reprinted with kind permission from *Psychology Today*. Please visit www.psychologytoday.com for further information.

Struggling children turn to bullying to cope

Children and young people struggling with personal issues are turning to bullying to help them cope according to a new survey.

The survey by anti-bullying charity Ditch the Label gathered responses from 8,850 12- to 20-year-olds on the subject of bullying. Of those surveyed half said they had been bullied, while a quarter of those who were bullied had resorted to bullying themselves.

Bullying as a response

The survey looked at the link between bullying and stress or trauma in the young people's lives. Of this link Ditch the Label say in their report:

"We were interested to see if bullying could be considered a behavioural response to stress or trauma. Our hypothesis was confirmed with very strong correlations – finding those who bully are more likely to experience stressful and/or traumatic situations than those who do not, suggesting it is a responsive behaviour."

On being a bully

For the report, the charity spoke to young people who had bullied others. One girl, now 18, said she

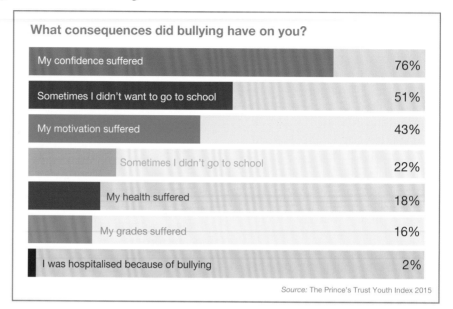

What consequences did bullying have on you?

My confidence suffered	76%
Sometimes I didn't want to go to school	51%
My motivation suffered	43%
Sometimes I didn't go to school	22%
My health suffered	18%
My grades suffered	16%
I was hospitalised because of bullying	2%

Source: The Prince's Trust Youth Index 2015

bullied a classmate for several years up until the age of 13. She now sees that this was a response to problems she was struggling with at home. She said:

"Bullying isn't just black and white, there are so many hidden things going on which lead to it happening and from what I've seen it's usually because the person doing the bullying is extremely unhappy and not confident within themselves. If I

could turn back time and undo it all I totally would."

Another young person, now 19, said:

"I bullied kids when I was at secondary school. Due to being very frustrated and unhappy with my life and myself."

Supporting young people

Nick Harrop, Media and Campaigns Manager at YoungMinds says bullying is a huge issue for young people. He said:

"Bullying can have a devastating impact on a child's life. It's important to ensure that young people, teachers and parents not only support those who've been bullied, but also work towards preventing it happening in the first place."

20 April 2016

⇨ The above information is reprinted with kind permission from Ditch the Label. Please visit www.ditchthelabel.org for further information.

Workplace bullying and harassment

Bullying and harassment are behaviours that makes someone feel intimidated or offended. Harassment is unlawful under the Equality Act 2010.

Examples of bullying or harassing behaviour include:

⇨ spreading malicious rumours

⇨ unfair treatment

⇨ picking on someone

⇨ regularly undermining a competent worker

⇨ denying someone's training or promotion opportunities.

Bullying and harassment can happen:

⇨ face-to-face

⇨ by letter

⇨ by e-mail

⇨ by phone.

The law

Bullying itself isn't against the law, but harassment is. This is when the unwanted behaviour is related to one of the following:

⇨ age

⇨ sex

⇨ disability

⇨ gender (including gender reassignment)

⇨ marriage and civil partnership

⇨ pregnancy and maternity

⇨ race

⇨ religion or belief

⇨ sexual orientation.

What employees should do if they're bullied or harassed

Employees should see if they can sort out the problem informally first. If they can't, they should talk to their:

⇨ manager

⇨ human resources (HR) department

⇨ trade union representative.

If this doesn't work, they can make a formal complaint using their employer's grievance procedure. If this doesn't work and they're still being harassed, they can take legal action at an employment tribunal.

They could also call the Acas (Advisory, Conciliation and Arbitration Service) helpline for advice.

Employers' responsibilities

Employers are responsible for preventing bullying and harassment – they're liable for any harassment suffered by their employees.

Anti-bullying and harassment policies can help prevent problems. Acas has produced a booklet for employers, including advice on setting up a policy as well as how to recognise, deal with and prevent bullying and harassment.

12 November 2014

⇨ The above information is reprinted with kind permission from GOV.UK. Please visit www.gov.uk for further information.

© Crown copyright 2016

Bullying in the workplace survey

Respondents to a Family Lives survey found those affected by workplace bullying saw a deterioration in relationships with partners, friends and family members.

Family Lives' survey respondents stated:

⇨ 91% felt that their organisation did not deal with the bullying adequately

⇨ 73% said the bullying was verbal, including threats, whereas 60% felt the bullying was social, including being excluded, ignored and isolated

⇨ 70% of survey respondents were female

⇨ 66% of respondents witnessed bullying at work with 43% stating they were bullied by their line manager, 38% bullied by a colleague and 20% bullied by SMT or CEO

⇨ 35% of bullying went on for more than a year.

Respondents quoted below reported that the anxiety associated with workplace bullying greatly affected their emotional health and wellbeing:

"I was blamed for errors made by other staff so work productivity greatly reduced as I was constantly checking database information that other staff compiled to ensure I was not blamed for any errors. I began taking work home to keep on top of my work but the more I managed, the more I was assigned, which made it impossible to make deadlines. I was requested to do work a certain way and then it was denied the request had been made. I became anxious, unable to eat and sleep dreaded going to work that I made myself ill until I was eventually diagnosed with anxiety and depression and work stress."

"Sent home after unfounded complaint received, never to return again. No procedures followed, no right of reply. Line manager said I admitted guilt when I hadn't. Denied any information. Procedures not followed. Ignored my request for an informal grievance against perpetrator. Ostracised for two months by all staff and trustees. Stress led me to having panic attacks and a full-blown tonic-clonic seizure. Secondment terminated. Suffered severe anxiety, and signed off sick for about 18 months. Have written professional evidence of being in positive mental health before this happened."

"It made and is making me depressed. Strangely, it's never affected my productivity because I have an unusually strong work ethic, and work more then I should. It's been more of a personal struggle, where I've gone from being a confident, strong individual to someone who's doing everything she can not to cry just writing this out. It has destroyed my self-esteem and my belief in myself."

"High level of anxiety daily. Led to panic attacks and PTSD. The workload became overbearing and was never completed well enough to satisfy the manager. Set up to fail daily."

"Affects my family life."

"As a contract worker, I am unable to challenge the behaviour because I worry my contract will not be renewed. Sleep loss. Anxiety attacks. Lack of self-worth. Unhappiness. Lack of confidence in my abilities. A desire to avoid work."

Jeremy Todd, Family Lives Chief Executive said:

"With New Year Resolutions firmly on the agenda, January is often the month when unsettled and distraught employees actively seek alternative employment. Our survey indicates this is often as a result of a breakdown in employee/employer relations. Family Lives recognises that workplace bullying is undoubtedly going to impact on family life. It would be very hard for anyone not to bring troubles home from work, but the pressure that a situation at work can put on relationships can make family life extremely turbulent. Support is out there and we would encourage people not to ignore incidents hoping that they will rectify themselves. The workplace should be an environment of professionalism, respect and courtesy and whilst many employers are committed to establishing a bullying-free zone, it is clear that work still needs to be done."

Particularly worrying data highlighted that:

⇨ 74% of respondents said that workplace bullying affected their family life and close relationships

⇨ 78% of respondents feel the financial climate and shortage of jobs is preventing individuals from standing up to workplace bullying

⇨ 48% felt that they need to continue to just put up with the bullying and 20% being signed off work with stress

⇨ 44% sought medical advice or counselling because of the bullying

⇨ 44% felt they needed to take official action to get the bullying to stop.

Quotes from survey respondents bullied by colleagues who felt that HR were not impartial or investigating issues or complaints from a neutral position included:

"HR are there to protect management and the organisation. You are made to feel a trouble causer!"

"If you make any waves, being on a nil-hours contract, it is easy for them to just give you no more work."

"Management are very weak and choose to ignore problems, bullying or otherwise, rather than to deal with them."

"The company is (a) small yet affluent business with under ten employees all of which have known each other for in excess of five years through the industry alone. There is no help, assistance, procedure for an 'outsider', openly discussing the issue creates more problems and more hatred and reaction and segregation."

"Complaint procedure inefficient. Too quick to listen to excuses from bully and put blame on victim (for) being too sensitive."

Family Lives' tips for employers who wish to tackle bullying in the workplace

⇨ Establishing an organisational culture dedicated to tackling bullying must be embedded in the Vision, Values and Aims of your organisation and be readily available via any existing staff handbook or HR resource. A bullying and harassment policy must be implemented and awareness of it widely disseminated via internal communication channels, making it clear that bullying behaviour will not be tolerated and those found guilty face disciplinary procedures

⇨ Educate employees via induction or awareness days on how to make a formal grievance, who they need to speak to (normally their manager) and what will happen after the incident has been reported

⇨ Provide examples of 'bullying behaviour' via any relevant staff handbook so that all staff are aware of their own behaviour and can take responsibility for it and are able to acknowledge that bullying can be verbal, non-verbal, written or physical

⇨ Anti-bullying policies must not be a 'tick box exercise' but reflect a real commitment to engendering a positive employee environment that is impartial towards all employees

⇨ Practical next steps include: training managers to recognise the traits and early signs of potential bullying and harassing behaviour. Encourage them to reflect on their management style as well as that of more forthright, dominant employers

⇨ Employers and employees should be encouraged to address issues concerning colleagues displaying possible signs of embryonic bullying behaviour before a situation escalates and becomes difficult for all parties to manage or achieve a workable resolution. While employers should encourage employees who feel they are being bullied to initially inform the offender that their tone or behaviour is unwelcome (by words or by conduct), this is not always possible

⇨ Ensure employees that all allegations of harassment or bullying will be taken seriously, confidentially and that grievances or complaints of harassment will not be ignored or treated lightly and will be investigated impartially and by external independent mediators if necessary.

Family Lives' key tips for employees who wish to tackle or address bullying in the workplace

⇨ All employees need to commit collectively and as individuals to a zero tolerance policy.

⇨ Be honest about your own behaviour, be prepared to report transgressions and actively support those that are bullied, don't hide behind a wall of silence and look the other way when abuses take place.

⇨ If ever we needed a policy of 'stand up and be counted' it is to combat bullying. Read more information from Acas on what to do about workplace bullying.

⇨ You can also talk to other people experiencing workplace bullying in our bullying forum.

⇨ Utilise the power of e-mail and following any perceived transgression, e-mail the person concerned calmly outlining your perception of what took place, what you had been asked to do/or criticised for not doing – this could also form part of a diary of incidents. It may also help the perpetrator to realise you are taking this seriously and will log all confrontational interactions – it will also help you to recollect exact times, dates and issues if a future grievance procedure takes place.

⇨ For those who are targeted by bullies, the worst feeling is that of helplessness. You can take control again:

- Firstly confide in someone you trust. Then keep a diary logging each and every incident that makes you feel belittled or afraid

- Note down the names of people who witnessed this. Hearsay evidence is not relevant, so this detail is really important

- Log what occurred but also how it made you feel. The writing of a diary is quite a cathartic experience in itself and empowers the employee by understanding that it is not them that has the problem, but the bully

- Contact a solicitor or union member if applicable.

Parents, adult carers and family members concerned about other family issues can call the free Family Lives helpline: 0808 800 2222 or visit http://familylives.org.uk/

12 January 2015

⇨ The above information is reprinted with kind permission from Family Lives. Please visit www.familylives.org.uk for further information.

Acas study reveals that workplace bullying is on the rise with many people too afraid to talk about it

A new Acas study published today reveals that workplace bullying is growing in Britain and many people are too afraid to speak up about it.

The Acas paper *Seeking better solutions: tackling bullying and ill-treatment in Britain's workplaces* looked at the latest research on workplace bullying as well as calls to the Acas helpline from employers and employees.

"Our analysis reveals that bullying is on the rise in Britain and it is more likely to be found in organisations that have poor workplace climates where this type of behaviour can become institutionalised."

Bullying and harassment are any unwanted behaviours that make someone feel intimidated, degraded, humiliated or offended. The Acas helpline has received around 20,000 calls related to bullying and harassment over the past year with some callers reporting that workplace bullying caused them to self-harm or consider suicide.

Acas Chair, Sir Brendan Barber, said:

"Our analysis reveals that bullying is on the rise in Britain and it is more likely to be found in organisations that have poor workplace climates where this type of behaviour can become institutionalised.

"Callers to our helpline have experienced some horrific incidents around bullying that have included humiliation, ostracism, verbal and physical abuse. But managers sometimes dismiss accusations around bullying as simply personality or management style clashes whilst others may recognise the problem but lack the confidence or skills to deal with it.

"Businesses should be taking workplace bullying very seriously as the annual economic impact of bullying-related absences, staff turnover and lost productivity is estimated to be almost £18 billion."

Acas' analysis showed that:

⇨ representative surveys of workplaces, health and safety representatives and employees all show that workplace bullying and ill-treatment is growing in Britain

⇨ there are more incidences of bullying within certain groups such as public sector minority ethnic workers; women in traditionally male-dominated occupations; workers with disabilities or long-term health problems; lesbian, gay and bisexual and transgender people; and workers in health care.

Calls to the Acas helpline around bullying revealed:

⇨ Barriers to people making complaints such as the fear that trying to do something about unwanted behaviour might make the situation worse.

⇨ Ill-treatment from other staff often built up to the point where people dreaded going to work, their family and home life had been affected and many took leave to escape the workplace.

⇨ Inexperienced employers can feel they lack the skills to go through complex grievance and disciplinary procedures that bullying allegations may involve.

⇨ Managers alerted to bullying allegations can favour simply moving staff around rather than investigating and dealing with underlying behaviours.

Brendan Barber added:

"Anti-bullying workplace policies and managers with good people management skills are essential to deal with the growing problem of bullying.

"Anti-bullying workplace policies and managers with good people management skills are essential to deal with the growing problem of bullying."

"Our study shows that encouraging a positive workplace climate is just as important as it allows people to have the confidence to report bullying when it occurs.

"This paper shines a light on workplace bullying with recommendations around how it can be tackled more effectively in the workplace."

The study recommends that workplaces agree standards of acceptable and unacceptable behaviours and senior leaders act as role models for these standards.

To see the full research report and Acas' guides for employers and employees on how to deal with bullying, please see *Bullying and harassment at work*.

16 November 2015

⇨ The above information is reprinted with kind permission from Acas. Please visit www.acas.org.uk for further information.

Bullying too often dismissed as "workplace banter"

More than a third of UK employees have been subjected to workplace bullying while a further fifth said they had witnessed a colleague being subjected to some form of abuse, according to research by employment law solicitors Slater and Gordon.

Examples of bullying as identified by the 2000 employees participating in the survey included shouting, shoving, intimidation and threatening behaviour. More than a quarter of those questioned had witnessed a colleague being deliberately humiliated by a bully and one in ten had heard racist insults. One in six had seen a co-worker subjected to inappropriate sexual remarks.

While most people had either been bullied at work or had seen a co-worker being bullied, less than half did anything about it. A third felt too awkward to confront the issue and a quarter thought it was simply part of the organisation's culture. A fifth thought they themselves would be the target of bullying if they spoke out and one in ten feared their job could be at risk if they complained.

What were often dismissed as "childish pranks" were observed by almost a quarter of respondents. One in 15 had witnessed a colleague's work being deliberately sabotaged and one in 20 had seen physical violence between workmates.

The research found that in more than half of cases bullying was disguised as "workplace banter". In many instances the behaviour was "subtle", such as deliberately not inviting a colleague out to work drinks, lunches and meetings. In a fifth of cases the victim was reduced to tears.

Of those who were themselves bullied, almost a third felt they had been humiliated in front of their co-workers. Almost a quarter said they had been shouted at by a colleague and one in ten had been deliberately excluded from social events. One in 20 had experienced objects being thrown at them.

According to the report, factors such as tight deadlines, personality clashes and office politics were often at the root of the problem.

Claire Dawson of Slater and Gordon said: "Bullying in the workplace is all too common and comes in many forms. The majority takes the shape of verbal abuse or intimidation. This is often dismissed as 'banter' between colleagues but the workplace shouldn't be a place where people are insulted. The idea that employees can be subjected to physical violence while at work is quite alarming. This can have a devastating impact on the person who is being bullied and can result in depression and anxiety.

"The research shows that most people who witness bullying prefer to do nothing about it. They are concerned for their own positions and aren't willing to put their necks on the line, especially when they don't know how an employer will respond.

"Our advice to anybody being bullied would be to stand up and take action. You have to confront the bully, either directly or through HR or a manager, to let them know that what they are doing is unacceptable."

"Office bullies must be banished from the workplace," added TUC general secretary Frances O'Grady. "The stress and anxiety felt by victims can make them physically ill, lose all self-confidence and mean that they dread coming into work. No one should be put in this position.

"Employers who fail to tackle bullying will pay a price too. Staff who are bullied are more likely to take time off because of the stress caused by their harassment and will be less productive at work."

The TUC said all organisations should have a workplace anti-bullying policy to tackle the problem. "Every employer should ensure that there is zero-tolerance of bullying either by line managers or workmates," stressed O'Grady.

25 August 2015

⇨ The above information is reprinted with kind permission from Health and Safety at Work. Please visit www.healthandsafetyatwork.com for further information.

Uh oh. Are you the workplace bully?

Five ways to tell and five reasons to stop right now.

By Bonnie Low-Kramen

In a recent Be the Ultimate Assistant workshop, we had "The Conversation". The topic was the global epidemic problem known as Workplace Bullying. In our class of 30 students, I asked, "How many of you have either witnessed or personally experienced workplace bullying?" As has happened in dozens of workshops and presentations all over the world, at least 50% of the students raised their hands. The fact is that they didn't even have to raise their hands for me to know the truth. Their eyes and body language said it all.

And then the stories began. Stories of assistants who quit their jobs because they couldn't take it any more. Stories of abusive managers who were eventually fired but who caused great trauma in the time they were at their companies. Stories of assistants who finally stand up to the bully after far too long a time and the relationship changes for the better. This painful but necessary segment in our BTUA workshop gives us the opportunity to shine a bright light on this toxic problem and the time to offer a great resource book for solutions: *Taming the Abrasive Manager* by Laura Crawshaw.

But the discussion didn't end there as it normally does. This time one of my students came up to me at a break with tears in her eyes and said, "I realise that I'm a bully to other assistants. Help me stop."

This is an aspect of workplace bullying that we hear less about and I applaud this student's willingness to look the problem squarely in the face – right in the mirror. The fact is that unless the pattern of bullying is broken through awareness, it has no reason to stop. Chances are that she is modelling behaviours that were inflicted on her. The abused often turn into abusers unless stopped.

> **"The fact is that unless the pattern of bullying is broken through awareness, it has no reason to stop."**

Whether the bully is a peer or a manager, the problem is taking a very big toll. Workplace bullying is traumatising humans and poisoning our companies from the inside out. Here is a very important point. The trauma from workplace bullying does not just last for the day it happens. The negative effects can last months and even years.

Very few people are trained on how to take on bullies, never mind successfully taking them on. No one wants to have these difficult conversations but have them we must. I can tell you that it can be done and when it happens, far fewer talented assistants feel forced to quit.

Answer these five questions to determine if you are a bully.

1. Have you yelled at someone today and on most days?
2. Do you intentionally withhold information and/or give others the 'silent treatment'?
3. Have you publicly humiliated and demoralised your colleagues by calling them morons, idiots and other disparaging epithets?
4. Do you throw things, stamp your feet, and pound your fist on the table to make your point?
5. Do you make fun of your peers with mean-spirited insults?

> **"Have you publicly humiliated and demoralised your colleagues by calling them morons, idiots and other disparaging epithets?"**

If three out of five answers were "Yes", here are the five reasons to alter your behaviour right now.

1. Because you behave with intimidation and fear, most everyone is afraid of speaking with you at all, never mind telling you important truths that you need to know. There is a lot that you are not being told about what is going on. No one seeks to be the dead messenger. Instead, your peers are doing everything they can to avoid you.
2. Staff who are respected and valued produce better work, are loyal, and go above and beyond when problems arise. The converse is true for staff who are disrespected, demeaned, and not acknowledged for the experience and talents that they were hired for in the first place. Your distracted and resentful peers may be physically there, but not really. The term is 'presenteeism'.
3. Your colleagues may be at their desks but many of them are busy looking for the exit – and they are doing it on company time.
4. Be honest. How many people are you bullying? Usually it is more than one. It is true that bullying takes the biggest toll on the victim but the witnesses of bullying also pay a high price, and they too will also look to quit. Have you heard of survivor's guilt?
5. Costs for employee sick time, litigation and replacing staff are skyrocketing. The word has gone around about how you treat people, so new staffers receive 'combat pay' just to take the job. Bullying is very expensive. Bullies get fired eventually because of this. The only question is when.

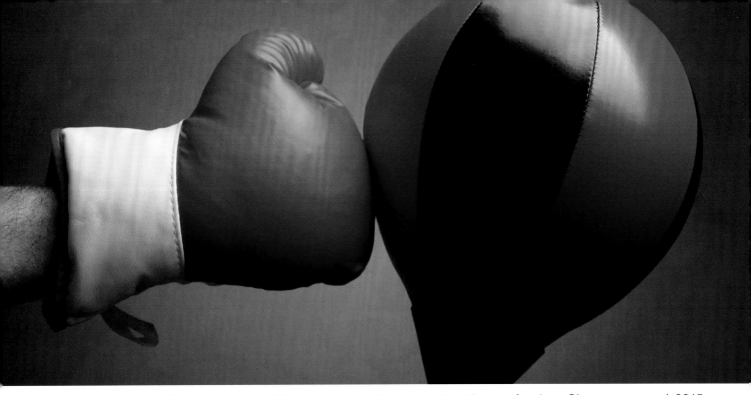

Convinced to turn things around? Here are five things to do about it.

1. Hire a counsellor or coach who specialises in bullying behaviours.
2. Have one-on-ones with your most trusted colleagues and friends and give them permission to tell you the truth. Really. Take notes.
3. Apologise to those you have hurt. Sincerity counts.
4. Speak with your HR Department to help them set realistic and actionable policies regarding bullying. Involve your colleagues in the creation of these policies and then ask to have them posted on the company website.
5. Encourage your peers to openly communicate with you as often as needed. Emphasise that they will not receive retribution.

"Workplace bullying can be stopped but it will take raising awareness by speaking up. We need to do it for ourselves and for those coming up behind us. There is much at stake."

Workplace bullying can be stopped but it will take raising awareness by speaking up. We need to do it for ourselves and for those coming up behind us. There is much at stake.

The bad news is that you have been a bully. The good news is that you made it to the end of this article in the hopes of finding the reasons to make a change. If you are still in doubt about whether you are a bully, just ask your colleagues. Their eyes will say it all.

About the author

Bonnie Low-Kramen is the Founder of Ultimate Assistant and is one of the most respected leaders in the administrative profession. She was named 2015 Educator of the Year by DEMA, the Domestic Estate Managers Association. The best-selling author of *Be the Ultimate Assistant*, she is known for her passionate commitment to being a catalyst for positive change in the global workplace. For 25 years, Bonnie worked as the Personal Assistant to Oscar winner Olympia Dukakis and now travels the world teaching and speaking. Clients include Starbucks, Amazon, AMC Entertainment, Dell and MasterCard. Bonnie co-hosts the monthly 'Be the Ultimate Assistant Podcast' with Vickie Sokol Evans available on iTunes. In the next 12 months, Bonnie will be at Executive Secretary LIVE in Dubai, Johannesburg and Auckland. For full details of the programmes and all the speakers please visit www.executivesecretarylive.com. She is a columnist for *Executive Secretary Magazine* and *SmartCEO Magazine*, and is a contributing writer to many other international publications. For more information visit www.bonnielowkramen.com.

Note: to view the original article, with American spellings, please visit http://executivesecretary.com/uh-oh-are-you-the-workplace-bully/.

25 March 2016

⇨ This article first appeared in *Executive Secretary Magazine*, a global training publication and must-read for any administrative professional. You can get a 30% discount when you subscribe through us. Visit the website at www.executivesecretary.com to find out more, or to get your 30% discount e-mail lbrazier@executivesecretary.com and tell them we sent you.

I am being bullied, what can I do?

Tell a friend

Your mates can support you, even if you're not ready to talk about it in detail. They can help take your mind off it and support you when you tell an adult you trust. Get support from other young people who are in the same situation as you on the bullying message board.

Tell a parent or guardian

They should be there for you, even if you're not ready to take it to your teachers. Find out more about asking an adult for help here: https://www.childline.org.uk/info-advice/you-your-body/getting-help/asking-adult-help.

Tell a teacher

The teachers in your school have a duty to look after you. You have a right to feel safe at school. Ask about the anti-bullying policy at your school – this should have details of what the school will do to tackle bullying.

Contact Childline

You can contact Childline for free on 0800 1111, anytime. Our counsellors are here to listen to you and can help you think of ideas to stop the bullying.

Find a way to stay safe at school

Nobody should be made to feel scared about going to school. You have a right to be there. Try to stay away from anyone who is involved in bullying and stay in a group of friends when you don't feel safe.

Walk home with someone or get a lift

If bullying happens on the way home, it might seem really hard to get away from it. Walking with someone, changing your route or getting a lift can help.

Ask your mates to look out for you

Your friends can be there for you, even if you don't want to talk about the details with them. They can support you to tell someone who could help make it stop.

Don't fight back

You could get in trouble or get hurt if you fight back against people involved in bullying. There's no shame in not fighting back.

Don't reply to an abusive message

Replying to an abusive message could make the bullying worse and might end up upsetting you more. It's a good idea to save these messages so that you can show them to a teacher or another adult.

Block the bully from contacting you

Some phones will let you block numbers. You can also block, delete or unfriend other users on lots of social networking sites. Stopping them from contacting you could help you feel less stressed and upset.

Find out about your school's anti-bullying policy

It's useful to know what your school has promised to do if bullying happens. There might be something in the policy that could help you.

Build your self-esteem

Experiencing bullying can knock anybody's confidence. A single

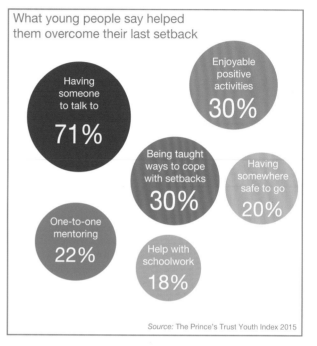

What young people say helped them overcome their last setback

Having someone to talk to **71%**

Enjoyable positive activities **30%**

Being taught ways to cope with setbacks **30%**

Having somewhere safe to go **20%**

One-to-one mentoring **22%**

Help with schoolwork **18%**

Source: The Prince's Trust Youth Index 2015

insult can stay with you for a long time. Sometimes you may even start believing that the insults are true – even though they aren't. Nobody deserves to be bullied and it isn't your fault that it is happening. It can happen to anybody.

Check out our video and tips on how you can build your confidence back up if you've experienced bullying. We also have advice about building your self-esteem: https://www.childline.org.uk/info-advice/your-feelings/feelings-emotions/building-confidence-self-esteem/.

My friend is being bullied, what can I do?

Be there for your friend

Sometimes your friend might not want to talk, but being there to listen whenever they are ready is important.

Help take their mind off it

Hanging out, going for a walk, watching a film or playing games together are good ways to take someone's mind off their problems for a little while.

Support your friend to help them speak out about bullying

Opening up to an adult about your problems can be scary. Going with a friend if they're feeling nervous is a great way to support them.

Help your friend stay safe at school

Staying in a group is a good way to help stop bullying during break times. You can also encourage your friend to talk to a teacher about what's going on.

Walk home with your friend or sit with them on the bus

It can be hard to get away from people involved in bullying when you are on the way to or from school. Walking with a friend and sitting in a group on the bus could help stop the bullying.

Speak to Childline about what is happening

You can talk to Childline, whatever your worry – even if you are worried about something that's happening to someone else.

Tell your friend about Childline

Make sure your friend knows that they can contact Childline any time, day or night, online or by phone. We're here to help.

Find out about your school's anti-bullying policy

It can help to know what your school has promised to do if bullying happens. There might be something in the policy that could help your friend.

⇨ The above information is reprinted with kind permission from Childline. Please visit www.childline.org.uk for further information.

Facebook leads the way against cyberbullying, but others need to follow

By Madhumita Murgia

This week Prince William joined the ranks of the tech-savvy royals when he attended Founders Forum, an invitation-only event for tech founders held at an 18th-century mansion in the depths of Hertfordshire.

Surrounded by the heads of Google, Facebook and Twitter, the Duke of Cambridge didn't choose to advocate for entrepreneurship or celebrate Britain's role in the digital revolution – instead he picked a surprisingly buzzword-free topic usually avoided at self-congratulatory events like these: cyberbullying.

The Prince said he had become "alarmed" by the rise of cyber trolls, particularly since becoming a parent, and called on social media giants to tackle bullying more actively. As a parent, he said, he was appalled at the news of teenage suicides and eating disorders borne out of online cruelty.

If there's any indication of how mainstream the issue has become, it's this. Last year, BullyingUK saw calls relating to cyberbullying increase by 77% over a 12-month period. In an online survey, BullyingUK also found that 43.5% of respondents aged between 11 and 16 had been bullied via social networks.

And while children are most vulnerable, adults and celebrities are equally exposed. Earlier this month, Uber's UK head Jo Bertram said she didn't use Twitter anymore because of the torrential abuse she received from black cab drivers who have compared her to Jimmy Saville, and also said they wished she would get run over by a car.

Monica Lewinsky, in her electric TED Talk about online shame, said that after her affair with President Bill Clinton became public, she almost lost her life to the "mobs of virtual stone-throwers" who publicly humiliated her for more than a decade.

The thing about online bullies is that they are faceless: on the web, gutless tormentors don't have to face up to their victims as they would in a school playground or in an office. Instead, they hide behind anonymous usernames and disappearing messages, a virtual mob loath to get their hands dirty.

It's time we brought some compassion to the Internet, but whose responsibility is it?

The average person has five social media accounts, and we spend almost 30% of our time online using these networks – about one hour and 40 minutes every day. Facebook is by far the largest online community, with 82% of the world's population, excluding China, having a Facebook account and 40% using it regularly. Twitter has roughly 350 million people signed up.

My opinion, like Prince William's, is that no one is better placed to encourage compassion than social media companies – after all, their networks have facilitated this new social phenomenon through their very existence. And it's not good enough just to solve a crime after it's committed – tech companies must start to police their vast virtual domains more proactively.

Back in 2013, a study suggested Facebook was the worst network for teenage cyberbullying; 87% of teens who reported cyber abuse said they were targeted on Facebook, while 20% blamed Twitter.

Despite its smaller size, Twitter has a particularly dark side, with harassment and trolling driving away even celebrity users, including

Stephen Fry and *The Great British Bake Off*'s Sue Perkins. Some believe it's the central reason that the platform is bleeding users.

Its former chief executive, Dick Costolo, made a very frank apology on an internal forum last year, admitting that the microblogging service "suck(s) at dealing with abuse and trolls on the platform and we've sucked at it for years".

The bare minimum responsibility would be to provide a channel for users to report direct abuse, threats and bullying. Last year, Twitter addressed this by allowing third parties to flag abuse rather than waiting for victims to do it themselves. It also broadened the criteria by which it assessed threats.

For example, where previously it would have required a troll to explicitly state details of a threat – such as wanting to commit sexual violence at the person's home – before it could act on it, it now acts on more generalised threats such as those of physical violence.

Last week, it also made it easier for users to block trolls effectively.

Facebook has been particularly driven in an effort to foster compassion within its vast network – one step forward from resolving complaints.

For example, take the 'reporting' tool on Facebook that allows you to report a photo or comment that you want taken down. To make people engage directly with each other and resolve conflict, Facebook's compassion team created take-down requests to communicate why the user wanted a post removed.

Human articulations such as "it's embarrassing" increased the requests hugely. And of those requests, 85% of the time, the person who posted the photo took it down or sent a reply, forcing bullies to talk directly to their victims.

Reporting abuse is the bedrock of online safety, but large social networks have to move to a more proactive form of compassion.

The most cutting-edge technologies such as machine learning are being used to make these products more fun, engaging and useful, but they could equally be applied to making these spaces more inclusive and empathetic.

For instance, hateful speech should be filtered by abuse-spotting algorithms and removed before it has the chance to inflict pain. Behavioural algorithms might be able to learn from profiles who is more likely to be a troll or a harasser and flag them up to community officers.

This week, Facebook took a big step in this direction by rolling out its Suicide Prevention tools globally. The Compassion team worked with 50 partners, including the Samaritans in Britain, to provide mental health resources for those at risk of suicide or self-harm.

The tool allows third parties to report posts that seemed like distress signals. If Facebook's large community monitoring team deems the reported post a cry for help, the person's normal Facebook experience will be paused when they next log in.

Instead, they will get a message saying one of their friends thought they might be going through a tough time, and an offer to help. Resources shared include contact details of local helplines, self-help tips and reminders of friends who could help. The person who reported the post receives a set of support resources as well.

For the most part, social networks, like the Internet itself, have been a unifying force, connecting everyone from angst-ridden teens to lonely grandparents around the world. Through them, we can engage with strangers, broadcast repressed ideas and ideologies, and record our lives for posterity.

But their immense scale also means social networks have got a finger on the pulse of humanity – the perfect vantage point from which to help. It's time they took their lead from the world's largest online community, and stepped up.

19 June 2016

⇨ The above information is reprinted with kind permission from *The Telegraph*. Please visit www.telegraph.co.uk for further information.

Duke of Cambridge announces plans to tackle cyberbullying

"The future of our children is inextricably linked with the Internet."

By Sarah Ann Harris

The Duke of Cambridge has announced an ambitious plan to bring together an industry-wide taskforce to tackle cyberbullying and support young people and their families affected by it.

William has asked Brent Hoberman, who founded lastminute.com with Martha Lane Fox in 1998, to chair the group which will be supported by The Royal Foundation of the Duke and Duchess of Cambridge and Prince Harry.

Over the coming year the Royal Foundation Taskforce on the Prevention of Cyberbullying will bring together industry partners and a group of advisers from the sector to develop an industry-wide response to the online bullying of young people, with a focus on 12- to 14-year-olds, the Press Association reports.

Hoberman said: "This taskforce will bring together the commitment, talent and expertise of the technology industry to tackle cyberbullying and the terrible effect it has on children.

"The future of our children is inextricably linked with the Internet. It is our responsibility to ensure that they grow up confident and happy online so that they can make the most of the extraordinary potential it offers."

The new initiative follows the announcement at the weekend that William, Kate and Harry want to "help change the national conversation" on mental health.

They are leading a campaign called Heads Together, which will be the biggest single project they have undertaken together.

It will be a partnership with charities with experience in tackling stigma, raising awareness, and providing help for people with mental health challenges.

A spokesman for the Duke of Cambridge said: "This is an issue that the Duke feels strongly about. He knows that social media and other technologies are creating significant positive opportunities for millions of young people.

"But as a parent, he knows that many people worry about how to protect their children from the new avenues for bullying that technology is creating.

"He hopes the taskforce can help the industry share the best practice that is emerging across the sector and put in place new standards so that the Internet remains something young people and their parents can embrace with confidence."

The spokesman added that while most social platforms and service providers do have systems in place for reporting or removing abusive content, there is no common industry standard or commitment to tackle the issue, nor is there an existing single repository of information for users on how to address it.

The taskforce will take existing models of good practice for reporting abusive content on individual networks and develop a set of commitments for the industry to sign up to, to collectively tackle the issue.

It will consider the development of a single resource of up-to-date practical support and information for young people affected by cyberbullying, with advice on how to get help. It will also work to help parents and adults to better understand cyberbullying, and give them the confidence to find appropriate help and resources to support children affected by the issue.

Kensington Palace said full membership of the taskforce would be announced soon and it will include leading figures from technology companies and Internet service providers.

The taskforce will also be supported by a panel of young people aged 11–15, to ensure it remains engaged in current online trends.

The Duchess of Cambridge also guest-edited a series on The Huffington Post UK earlier this year, looking at the importance of looking after the mental health of young children.

28 April 2016

⇨ The above information is reprinted with kind permission from The Huffington Post UK. Please visit www.huffingtonpost.co.uk for further information.

Cyberbullying – top tips for young people

1. Always respect others: be careful what you say online and what images you send.

2. Think before you send: whatever you send can be made public very quickly and could stay online forever.

3. Keep it private! Only give your mobile number, personal e-mail address and other contact details to trusted friends. If you are active on social networking services think about what you are sharing and who you are sharing it with. You can set your privacy settings to limit who can see your content.

4. Block the bully: learn how to block or report someone who is behaving badly.

5. Don't retaliate or reply!

6. Save the evidence: learn how to keep records of upsetting or mean messages, pictures or online conversations.

7. Make sure you tell:

    • Your parent/carer or an adult you trust.

    • Your school: your teacher or the anti-bullying coordinator can help you

    • Report it to the social network or app: you can check their help centre to see where to report concerns

    • Remember you can visit Childline to chat to a counsellor online, or call 0800 1111.

8. Finally, don't just stand there, if you see cyberbullying going on, support the victim and report the bullying!

17 November 2015

⇨ The above information is reprinted with kind permission from Childnet International. Please visit www.childnet.com for further information.

© Childnet International 2016

Preventing bullying with emotional intelligence

***An article from* The Conversation.**

THE CONVERSATION

By Marc Brackett, Senior Research Scientist in Psychology, Yale University and Susan Rivers, Psychology Research Scientist, Yale University

In school, emotions matter. Not only do children with anxiety and aggression have difficulty focusing and learning, they also tend to be victims or perpetrators of bullying. Whether it's old-fashioned physical or verbal aggression, ostracism, or online abuse, bullying is deeply rooted in a lack of emotional intelligence skills. These skills can and should be taught, though they seldom are.

What kids need is a curriculum in emotional intelligence skills. These include the ability to recognise emotions in the self and in others; understand the causes of emotions and their consequences for thinking and behaviour; label emotions with a sophisticated vocabulary; express emotions in socially appropriate ways; and regulate emotions effectively. Emotionally intelligent people of all ages recognise a healthy range of emotions in themselves and others – insight that helps them to form stable, supportive relationships and enjoy greater wellbeing and academic or job performance.

Emotional intelligence protects people from depression, anxiety and aggression, and equips them to face bullying by managing their own fear and reaching out for help. By contrast, a lack of emotional intelligence predicts aggression, substance abuse and worse mental health.

Teaching emotional intelligence, while quite feasible, isn't as simple as adding a subject to the schedule. On the contrary, a successful emotional curriculum takes a whole-school approach. It begins by educating teachers, administrators and parents, for many of whom these skills will be new. Only after that are the concepts introduced to students.

In the United States, some 500 schools have introduced an evidence-based programme called RULER, designed to teach the skills for recognising, understanding, labelling, expressing, and regulating emotions.

RULER uses four anchors of emotional intelligence upon which a flexible emotional intelligence curriculum is built. Students and teachers write collaborative Charters detailing the behaviours they expect from one another. They learn to locate feelings on a Mood Meter and gain a rich vocabulary to describe those feelings. They are taught to take a Meta-Moment – a short pause – before reacting to provocation. And they devise a blueprint to address problem behaviours that do arise.

The results of RULER training are strikingly positive. In RULER schools, focus and classroom climate improves. Students and teachers form better relationships, and teachers suffer less burnout. Children are less anxious and depressed and do better academically, as well as showing greater social skills and fewer behavioural problems. Suspensions can fall by as much as 60%. And bullying decreases.

In the US, a federal bill is under consideration that would support adding social-emotional learning to teacher-training programmes.

A system-wide, evidence-based education in emotional intelligence is every bit as important as an education in traditional subjects. By contrast, failing to offer children these crucial skills creates a fertile environment for bullying. Australia's children deserve an emotional education, one that gives them every chance to become more effective learners and happier, more self-aware and more compassionate human beings.

That's what Victoria's Girton Grammar School in Bendigo did in 2011. It sent teachers to the US to be trained in RULER, subsequently becoming the country's first to adopt the programme.

Melbourne's King David School and a handful of other Victorian and NSW schools have adopted the programme as well. KidsMatter Primary is a Department of Health-funded social and emotional learning programme built on similar principles; the schools it has reached include those in disadvantaged areas, such as Coolaroo South Primary School in northern Victoria – places where, arguably, children may benefit even further from an understanding of emotion.

Bullying is a major problem in Australia. The Australian Covert Bullying Prevalence study found that over one in four children in Years 4 to 9 reported being bullied

at least every few weeks, with hurtful teasing and lies the most common behaviours. In 2008, a tenth of Aboriginal and Torres Strait Islander children between the ages of four and 14 reported being bullied in school about their Indigenous origins.

Bullying victims suffer higher rates of depression, anxiety, social withdrawal and suicidal thoughts. They also do worse academically. Perpetrators suffer, too, experiencing more depression, anxiety, hostility and substance abuse. Even children who are bystanders may be traumatised. Worst off are bully-victims – kids who are both bullying victims and bullies in their own right. As adults, this group often goes on to criminal behaviour and partner abuse.

The United States has made many well-meaning attempts to legislate bullying out of existence, introducing measures like zero-tolerance policies, close monitoring and awareness assemblies. But bullying rates haven't dropped. Such law-and-order approaches can even backfire when children

taught to stand up to bullies face retaliation.

The programmes fail because get-tough strategies neglect to address the reasons children bully: namely, a lack of emotional understanding and an inability to self-regulate powerful emotions. Children who don't know what to do with emotions like frustration, fear or isolation may turn to bullying for emotional release. If we teach our children to be emotionally intelligent, they'll learn how to recognise these emotions and transform them into something more positive.

11 May 2014

⇨ The above information is reprinted with kind permission from *The Conversation*. Please visit www.theconversation.com for further information.

Teacher uses two apples to perfectly illustrate the emotional impact of bullying on children

Couldn't have put it better ourselves.

By Amy Packham

A teacher perfectly illustrated the damaging effect bullying can have on kids using two red apples.

Prior to her lesson, the teacher from Staffordshire had repeatedly dropped one of the apples on the floor, bruising its flesh but without damaging the outside.

In class, the children discussed how both the apples looked the same on the outside – both red and a similar size.

"I picked up the apple I'd dropped on the floor and started to tell the children how I disliked this apple, that I thought it was disgusting, it was a horrible colour and the stem was just too short," the teacher wrote on a post on the Relax Kids Tamworth Facebook page.

"I told them that because I didn't like it, I didn't want them to like it either, so they should call it names too.

"Some children looked at me like I was insane, but we passed the apple around the circle calling it names, 'You're a smelly apple', 'I don't even know why you exist', 'You've probably got worms inside you'."

With the kids still unaware what was going on, the teacher proceeded to pass around the other apple and asked the kids to say kind words about it.

The children called the apple "lovely", with "beautiful skin" and a "beautiful colour".

The teacher continued: "I then held up both apples, and again, we talked about the similarities and differences, there was no change, both apples still looked the same.

"I then cut the apples open. The apple we'd been kind to was clear, fresh and juicy inside.

"The apple we'd said unkind words to was bruised and all mushy inside."

The teacher said there was a "light bulb" moment for the children immediately.

"They really got it, what we saw inside that apple, the bruises, the mush and the broken bits is what is happening inside every one of us when someone mistreats us with their words or actions," she wrote.

"When people are bullied, especially children, they feel horrible inside and sometimes don't show or tell others how they are feeling.

"If we hadn't have cut that apple open, we would never have known how much pain we had caused it.

"More and more hurt and damage happens inside if nobody does anything to stop the bullying. Let's create a generation of kind, caring children.

"The tongue has no bones, but is strong enough to break a heart. So be careful with your words."

The teacher's post was shared nearly 80,000 times on Facebook, garnering an impressive 72,000 likes and 8,000 comments, all in just 18 hours.

Commenters praised her "innovative" way of illustrating bullying to children.

22 June 2016

⇨ The above information is reprinted with kind permission from The Huffington Post UK. Please visit www.huffingtonpost.co.uk for further information.

Bullying in school plummets

New study reveals 30,000 fewer children bullied in last ten years.

Bullying and violence in English schools has plummeted in the last decade, a major new study has revealed.

The landmark study involving more than 10,000 secondary school pupils shows that:

⇨ 30,000 fewer children in England now face the fear of bullying compared to 2005

⇨ robbery between pupils has halved – last year just 1% of children reported being robbed.

The new figures come as part of the Government's continued drive to deliver an excellent education for every child – and make sure teachers have the tools they need to tackle bullying and violence in schools.

A range of tough new powers have been introduced since 2010 to enable heads and teachers to retake control of their classrooms. On top of this, the Government has pledged to train every teacher in not just how to tackle serious behaviour issues, but how to deal with low-level disruption that stops children from learning properly.

Strengthened measures already in use in our classrooms include:

⇨ stronger powers to search pupils

⇨ removing the requirement to give parents 24-hours' written notice of after-school detentions

⇨ clarifying teachers' power to use reasonable force to control unruly pupils.

Teachers also now have greater powers to tackle cyberbullying by searching for and deleting inappropriate images on mobile phones and tablets. In addition, £3.3 million is being made available this year to charitable organisations to help tackle bullying and provide support for those who are bullied. This is on top of the £4 million provided in 2013 to 2015.

Speaking before the launch of Anti-Bullying Week, Education Secretary Nicky Morgan hailed the new figures, suggesting that getting tough on discipline, creating a climate of tolerance and supporting bullied children can change lives for the better. She said:

"As part of our commitment to delivering social justice we are helping teachers and charities end the scourge of bullying in our schools. We are determined to tackle any barriers which stop pupils attending school and learning so they can fulfil their potential.

"Thanks to our reforms and their efforts, bullying is plummeting. While there is still more to do, today's news confirms that strong discipline coupled with the right support allows children to flourish, and can transform lives by reducing bullying."

A 2014 report by Stonewall also showed that homophobic bullying has fallen, with the number of secondary school teachers who say their pupils are often or very often the victim of homophobic bullying has almost halved since 2009. To further tackle this, the Government has announced a £2 million fund for projects to address homophobic, biphobic and transphobic bullying in schools.

The Government has a package of measures to help schools tackle bullying and encourage good behaviour so that children can learn in a safe environment, free from fear and harm. This includes:

⇨ placing a greater focus on behaviour and bullying in school inspections

⇨ appointing behaviour expert Tom Bennett to lead a review to ensure new teachers are fully trained in dealing with disruptive children and consider all of the challenges of managing behaviour in 21st-century schools

⇨ strengthening teachers' powers to tackle bullying – this includes the power to investigate allegations beyond the school gates, delete inappropriate images from phones and give out same-day detention

⇨ launching a £2 million fund for projects to build schools' knowledge and capacity to prevent and tackle homophobic, biphobic and transphobic bullying in schools

⇨ awarding around £1.3 million over 12 months from April 2015 to three anti-bullying organisations, including the Diana Award, Kidscape and the National Children's Bureau, to extend their work supporting schools to combat bullying

⇨ providing £4 million in 2013 to 2015 to anti-bullying charities to help schools develop strategies to tackle bullying, including £1.5 million for the National Children's Bureau consortium to focus on children and young people with special educational needs who are bullied

⇨ ensuring that children are better educated about the dangers of the Internet – children are now learning about Internet safety as part of the new national curriculum, and Safer Internet Day is widely promoted each year.

15 November 2015

⇨ The above information is reprinted with kind permission from the Department for Education. Please visit www.gov.uk for further information.

Key facts

- 50% of young people have bullied another person, 30% of which do it at least once a week. (page 3)

- 69% of young people have witnessed somebody else being bullied, 43% of which see it at least once a week. (page 3)

- 43% of young people have been bullied, 44% of which are bullied at least once a week. (page 3)

- Appearance is cited as the number one aggressor of bullying, with 51% saying they were bullied because of attitudes towards how they look. (page 3)

- 26% said their weight was targeted, 21% body shape, 18% clothing, 14% facial features, 9% glasses and 8% hair colour. (page 3)

- 23% of females with ginger hair cited their hair colour as the bullying aggressor. (page 3)

- Overall, 47% of young people want to change their appearance. 48% want teeth whitening, 17% breast implants, 6% liposuction and 5% Botox. (page 3)

- 74% of those who have been bullied, have, at some point, been physically attacked. 17% have been sexually assaulted. 62% have been cyber bullied. (page 3)

- As a result of bullying, 29% self-harmed, 27% skipped class, 14% developed an eating disorder and 12% ran away from home. (page 3)

- 41% of people believe that bullying has always been rife and that cyberbullying is simply another channel. (page 5)

- 85% of parents of disabled children who had been bullied believed they were targeted because of their disability, according to one online survey. (page 7)

- A study of 4,200 students from North Carolina found the likelihood of victimisation increased by 25% when a typical student climbed to the top 5% of the social hierarchy. (page 9)

- Homophobic bullying is the most frequent form of bullying after name calling. According to Stonewall's School report, 96% of gay pupils hear homophobic remarks such as 'poof' or 'lezza' used in school.

- 99% hear phrases such as 'that's so gay' or 'you're so gay' in school. (page 11)

- 51% of respondents to Ditch The Label's Annual Bullying Survey believe they were bullied because of their appearance, while 23% believed it was because of their high grades. 15% said they were bullied because of attitudes to household income. (page 13)

- 94% of young people who were bullied were verbally/emotionally abused. 23% were physically attacked. 13% were abused online. (page 18)

- A recent study found that the most common type of bullying is name calling – 36% experienced this, while 23% had belongings taken. The same study found that most teenagers never told a teacher (41%–74%) or a parent (24%–51%), but up to 75% told an adult about physical bullying such as being hit or beaten up. (page 21)

- Research has shown that by the age of 24, bullies are 60% more likely to have a criminal record than any other group. (page 22)

- 76% of young people who were bullied said that it affected their confidence. 51% said that sometimes they didn't want to go to school because of it, and 2% said they were hospitalised because of being bullying. (page 24)

- A recent Family Lives survey regarding bullying in the workplace found that:
  - 91% felt that their organisation did not deal with the bullying adequately
  - 73% said the bullying was verbal, including threats, whereas 60% felt the bullying was social, including being excluded, ignored and isolated
  - 70% of survey respondents were female
  - 66% of respondents witnessed bullying at work with 43% stating they were bullied by their line manager, 38% bullied by a colleague and 20% bullied by SMT or CEO
  - 35% of bullying went on for more than a year. (page 26)

- 71% of young people said having someone to talk to helped them overcome their last setback. (page 32)

- Last year, BullyingUK saw calls relating to cyberbullying increase by 77% over a 12-month period. (page 33)

Bullying

A form of aggressive behaviour used to intimidate someone. It can be inflected both physically and mentally (psychologically).

Communications Act 2003

The Communications Act 2003 governs the Internet, e-mail, mobile phone calls and text messaging. This means that it is an offence to send messages or other matter that are 'grossly offensive or of an indecent, obscene or menacing character', whether the targeted person actually sees the message or not.

Cyberbullying

Cyberbullying is when technology is used to harass, embarrass or threaten to hurt someone. A lot is done through social networking sites such as Facebook and Twitter. Bullying via mobile phones is also a form of cyberbullying. With the use of technology on the rise, there are more and more incidents of cyberbullying.

Discrimination

Unfair treatment against someone because of the group/class they belong too.

Harassment

Usually persistent (but not always), a behaviour that is intended to cause distress and offence. It can occur on the school playground, in the workplace and even at home.

Homophobic bullying

Homophobia is the fear or hatred of people who are attracted to the same sex as themselves (e.g. disliking lesbians, gay men and bisexuals). This form of bullying is slightly different because of the personal motivation that drives it, in this case being directed at someone who is gay, lesbian or thought to be by others.

Non-verbal abuse

Can be thought of as a kind of 'psychological warfare' because instead of using spoken words or direct physical violent behaviour, this form of abuse involves the use of mimicry (teasing someone by mimicking them), offensive gestures or body language.

Racist bullying

Targeting a person because of their race, colour or beliefs. There is a difference between racism and racial harassment: racial harassment refers to words and actions that are intentionally said/done to make the target feel small and degraded due to their race or ethnicity.

Self-harm/self-injury

Self-harm is the act of deliberately injuring or mutilating oneself. People injure themselves in many different ways, including cutting, burning, poisoning or hitting parts of their body. Self-harmers often see harming as a coping strategy and give a variety of motivations for hurting themselves, including relieving stress or anxiety, focusing emotional pain and as a way of feeling in control. Although prevalent in young people, self-harm is found amongst patients of all ages. It is not usually an attempt to commit suicide, although people who self-harm are statistically more likely to take their own lives than those who don't.

Sexual bullying

This includes a range of behaviours such as sexualised name-calling and verbal abuse, mocking someone's sexual performance, ridiculing physical appearance, criticising sexual behaviour, spreading rumours about someone's sexuality or about sexual experiences they have had or not had, unwanted touching and physical assault. Sexual bullying is behaviour which is repeated over time and intends to victimise someone by using their gender, sexuality or sexual (in)experience to hurt them.

Social media

Media which are designed specifically for electronic communication. `Social networking' websites allow users to interact using instant messaging, share information, photos and videos and ultimately create an online community. Examples include Facebook, LinkedIn and micro-blogging site Twitter.

Troll/Troller

Troll is Internet slang for someone who intentional posts something online to provoke a reaction. The idea behind the trolling phenomenon is that it is about humour, mischief, and some argue, freedom of speech; it can be anything from a cheeky remark to a violent threat. However, sometimes these Internet pranks can be taken too far, such as a person who defaces Internet tributes site, causing the victims family further grief.

Verbal abuse

Spoken words out loud intended to cause harm, such as suggestive remarks, jokes or name calling.

Assignments

Brainstorming

⇨ In small groups, discuss what you know about bullying:

- What kinds of bullying are there?

- Why do people bully?

- Where can bullying take place?

Research

⇨ Create an anonymous questionnaire that will be distributed throughout your year group, to find out how many people have experience of bullying. Decide whether you want to focus on people who have been bullied, or people who are bullies. Then work with a partner to construct at least ten questions. Distribute your questionnaire, thinking carefully about how people will return it anonymously, then gather your results and create a presentation for your class, including graphs and infographics if appropriate.

⇨ Talk to some adults you know about their experiences of bullying in the workplace. Have they witnessed workplace bullying? What are the differences between school bullies and work bullies? Write some notes and then feed back to your class.

⇨ Use the Internet to research anti-bullying campaigns. Choose one you think is effective or original and discuss with a classmate.

⇨ Speak to an adult you know about their experiences of childhood bullying. Ask them about the long-term effects and then talk through your findings with the rest of your class.

Design

⇨ In small groups, design a school-based campaign that will highlight the effects of bullying. You should choose one particular type of bullying for your campaign – cyberbullying, emotional, verbal or physical. You could use posters, articles in your school newspaper, assemblies or even a website. Be creative!

⇨ Imagine you work for a company that is experiencing problems with workplace bullying among its staff. Create an engaging e-mail that will highlight the issue, including advice for anyone who is affected.

⇨ Design a horizontal banner that could be displayed as an advert on websites to highlight the effects of cyberbullying.

⇨ Choose one of the articles from this book and create an illustration that highlights the key themes of the piece.

Oral

⇨ Imagine that you are concerned about your friend because you think he/she is being bullied. Write an e-mail to your friend explaining why you are concerned and giving advice about where they could turn for help.

⇨ Read the article *Girl bullies "could be great leaders", says expert* on page 15. Do you agree with this article? Do you think it is making unfair links between girls who bully and girls who are assertive/'fiery'. Do you concur with the statement 'many great leaders have had a tendency towards bullying behaviour'? Discuss as a class.

⇨ In pairs, go through this book and discuss the cartoons you come across. Think about what the artists were trying to portray with each illustration.

⇨ Create a PowerPoint presentation that explains the myths and facts surrounding the issue of bullying.

⇨ In pairs, discuss the long-term effects of bullying.

⇨ According to the article on page 18, victims of bullying are more likely to suffer from nightmares (*Bully victims more likely to suffer night terrors and nightmares*). In pairs, list as many of the physical and mental effects of bullying as you can think of, then feed back to your class.

⇨ 'Calling someone names doesn't hurt them as much as hitting them.' Discuss this statement in small groups and feed back to your class.

Reading/writing

⇨ Read the article *Why bullies don't feel bad (or don't know they do)* on page 23 and write a summary for your school newspaper.

⇨ Watch the film *Cyberbully*, starring Masie Williams. Write a review discussing the film's portrayal of bullying and bullies.

⇨ In the article on page 38, a teacher used apples to demonstrate the emotional effects of bullying. Write an innovative lesson plan that could also be used to explain these effects to students aged seven.

Acknowledgements

The publisher is grateful for permission to reproduce the material in this book. While every care has been taken to trace and acknowledge copyright, the publisher tenders its apology for any accidental infringement or where copyright has proved untraceable. The publisher would be pleased to come to a suitable arrangement in any such case with the rightful owner.

Images

All images courtesy of iStock, except page 10 © Corina Ardenleanu and page 38: Pixabay.

Illustrations

Don Hatcher: pages 13 & 18. Simon Kneebone: pages 3 & 24. Angelo Madrid: pages 8 & 29.

Additional acknowledgements

Editorial on behalf of Independence Educational Publishers by Cara Acred.

With thanks to the Independence team: Mary Chapman, Sandra Dennis, Christina Hughes, Jackie Staines and Jan Sunderland.

Cara Acred

Cambridge

September 2016